Natural Law

Natural Law

An Introduction and Re-examination

HOWARD P. KAINZ

OPEN COURT
Chicago and La Salle, Illinois

To order books from Open Court, call toll-free 1-800-815-2280, or visit our website at www.opencourtbooks.com.

Open Court Publishing Company is a division of Carus Publishing Company.

Printed and bound in the United States of America.

Library of Congress Cataloging-in-Publication Data

Kainz, Howard P.
    Natural law : an introduction and re-examination / Howard P. Kainz.
        p. cm.
    Includes bibliographical references and index.
    ISBN 0-8126-9454-6 (trade paper : alk. paper)
    1. Ethics. 2. Natural law. I. Title.
BJ1012.K264 2004
171'.2--dc22

                                                                2004010796

For Erika

Contents

Introduction

He who bids the law rule may be deemed to bid God and Reason alone rule, but he who bids man rule adds an element of the beast; for desire is a wild beast, and passion perverts the minds of rulers, even when they are the best of men. The law is reason unaffected by desire. . . . Customary [unwritten] laws have more weight, and relate to more important matters, than written laws, and a man may be a safer ruler than the written law, but not safer than the customary law.

— ARISTOTLE, *Politics* III, 1287a, b

In April 1996 I attended a conference on "Natural Law and Contemporary Public Policy" at the Cleveland-Marshall College of Law in Cleveland. I immediately sensed that this conference was different from the other philosophy conferences I had attended, since I was the only person there not wearing a tie. The speakers and most participants at the conference were lawyers and judges and law students; I met only a couple of fellow philosophers there. I was able to borrow a nondescript tie from a bellman at my hotel, and as I attended the sessions made a few further discoveries. For one thing, the lawyers were referring to themselves as "natural lawyers"—an expression I had for some reason never before encountered—and they seemed to feel comfortable with that title, although to me it sounded a bit awkward and could have multiple meanings (as contrasted, for example, with "trained lawyers" or "contrived lawyers" or "metaphysical lawyers," as well as "positivistic lawyers"). But more importantly, in the presentations by various speakers the emphasis on the practical—applications to tort reform, privacy, welfare, divorce, pornography, abortion, *in vitro* fertilization, euthanasia, assisted suicide, workplace safety, school choice, homosexuality, sodomy, taxation, the right or duty to work, just-war theory, and other contemporary moral issues.[1] I hesitate to refer to these as "applications of *natural law*" without qualification, since the applications in question were of a wide variety of natural-law theories, or would-be natural-law theories (more on this in the chapters that follow). The theorists mentioned included Aristotle, Plato, the Stoics, Aquinas, Suarez, Hobbes, Locke, Grotius, Pufendorf, and Kant (!), as well as Grisez and Finnis and other spokespersons for the "New Natural Law Theory" that has sparked significant contemporary interest among ethicists.

Issuing from this *Who's Who* and *Who Was Who* of theorists there are clearly major differences in the approaches and presuppositions and tenets, so that it would seem to be oversimplifying and misleading to talk about multiple applications of "the" natural law. Or is there some sort of intuitively clear bedrock meaning in natural law, aspects of which can be brought out to a greater or lesser degree by the various theorists? One thinks of the various "natural law" movements taking place now—branches of the Natural Law Party in the U.S., Canada, Great Britain, Israel, New Zealand, and Pakistan as well as Mothers for Natural Law and similar organizations, which have by no means tried to arrive at a consensus about what is *meant* by natural law, or about which theory offers the best expression of natural law. Possibly the situation with natural law is similar to the famous statement about pornography made by Justice Potter Stewart, who in his concurring opinion to the Supreme Court's decision in *Jebollis v. Ohio* (1964) wrote that while he could not define hard-core pornography, "I know it when I see it."

But my impression is that what Justice Potter meant was that he had a general, difficult-to-define, sense about what is moral and what is not; and that this is also what is meant by most organizations with the "natural law" tag. In other words, the term, "natural law," can be used by some persons as a code-word to indicate a return to morality,

---

[1] The papers from these sessions have since been published. See David F. Forte, ed., *Natural Law and Contemporary Public Policy* (Washington, D.C.: Georgetown University Press 1998).

or a coordination of morality with politics, or culture, or everyday life. But certainly the natural lawyers, who are well acquainted with various versions of natural-law theory, do not simply equate natural law with morality.

Professional philosophers find many subtle and not-so-subtle differences among various ethical theories; and natural-law theories, at present a minority contender for interest among ethicists, is thought to be quite divergent from other ethical theories—partly because of their *prima facie* divergent multiplicity, partly because some of the theories seem to be based on an inadmissible fusion of nature and morality, or are based on *a priori* or overly abstruse principles. Some also criticize natural law as being too closely connected with religion, in the sense that the magisterium of the Catholic Church and Catholic "scholastic" philosophers have traditionally promoted natural law as the paramount moral theory.

In the twentieth century the Nuremberg Trials after World War II provided a major impetus for a revival of interest in natural law. Since the Nazi officers and officials accused of war crimes or crimes against humanity in this trial were very often simply following orders, and acting within the parameters of legality prevailing during the Third Reich, the obvious question emerged: By what right, on what authority, could the judges in this trial convict the defendants for their crimes? Is there some higher law, or are there some fundamental— possibly implicit or unwritten—laws, in the light of which enacted valid positive laws of a nation can be judged unjust, invalid, and nonbinding, such that any rational citizen putatively subject to these laws would have no duty to obey them, and even a serious obligation to disobey them? If a convicted criminal is subject to capital punishment for *obeying* laws, the laws governing the conviction should be clear, unambiguous and command a public assent tantamount to what ordinarily goes under the name of "promulgation."

In the aftermath of Nuremberg, legal scholars began to respond to concerns about the validity of laws—whether, for example, an immoral law, passed according to constitutional procedures in a country, would be binding. Legal positivist H.L.A. Hart defended the validity of even "bad" laws in his 1957 Holmes Lecture at Harvard Law School, the publication of which led to a debate with fellow Harvard professor Lon Fuller in the pages of the *Harvard Law Review*, and further books and articles; the debate was eventually joined by Yale professor Ronald Dworkin.[2] Although Hart recognizes that moral principles are often incorporated in legislative enactments, and allows for a "minimum content" of natural law in these enactments,[3] Fuller and Dworkin have argued for a more extensive relationship between morality and law, and have been credited with a defense of "natural law" in the wide sense.

The task of natural-law theory can be interpreted as arguing that there do exist some supervening meta-laws, or as working toward a clarification of such laws, or as the specification of just what the laws are. The number of books on natural law has been growing each decade. According to the *World Catalogue*, 282 books on the subject "natural law" were published during the 1950s, 486 during the 1960s, 493 during the 1970s, 557 during the 1980s, and 694 during the 1990s. Under the auspices of the School of Law at Notre Dame, the journal, *Natural Law Forum* was established in the 1950s, continuing under the title, *American Journal of Jurisprudence* after 1968. Another journal, *Vera Lex,* published under the auspices of the International Natural Law Society, has since 1980 published wide-ranging articles from public and private, religious and secular, colleges, and from professionals outside of academics as well as academic authors. Articles on various aspects of natural law appear frequently in other journals in philosophy, politics, law and economics.

During the 1960s an additional impetus towards a renewed interest in, or reaction against, natural law, arose from the publication of Pope Paul VI's encyclical letter *Humanae vitae*, in which the Pope supported his opposition to artificial contraception by appealing to Thomistic natural-law theory as well to religious or theological considerations. The predictable reactions by proponents of birth control against the papal pronouncement were complemented by arguments by ethicists against the very idea of natural law, which could lead to allegedly idiosyncratic interpretations of human sexuality. But Catholic moralists such as Germain Grisez and John Finnis came to

---

[2] Writings emerging from this debate include H.L.A. Hart, *The Concept of Law* (Oxford: Clarendon, 1961); Lon Fuller, *The Morality of Law* (New Haven: Yale University Press,1969), and Ronald Dworkin, "Morality and Law: Observations Prompted by Professor Fuller's Novel Claim," *University of Pennsylvania Law Review* (1965), 668–690.

[3] See below, page 45.

the Pope's defense,[4] developing "natural law" arguments against contraception, as well as against homosexuality, abortion, and other issues on which the Church had taken a stand. Finnis's book, *Natural Law and Natural Rights*,[5] initially inspired by a 1965 article by Germain Grisez,[6] offered a systematic and comprehensive defense of a theory which has become known as the "new natural-law theory." This theory has been subsequently shored up and defended by Robert George,[7] Joseph Boyle, and others; but also has been subjected to considerable criticism by natural-law ethicists from the Thomistic tradition, including Ralph McInerny,[8] Henry Veatch,[9] and Russell Hittinger.[10] Questions have been raised about the connection of the "new natural-law theory" with the traditional natural-law theory, and in particular with the Thomistic concept of natural law. The ongoing debate about the new theory will be considered in Chapter 4.

In a previous book,[11] I characterized natural-law theory as one of a group of theories that emphasize the objectivity of morality, which is to say that there are a least a subset of moral norms that are not merely the products or creations of subjective viewpoints or to be judged by subjective intentions, but based in human nature, the nature of society, or evolving nature. In the present book, focusing specifically on the evolution of the notion of an objective morality based in human nature, the first four chapters examine major historical milestones. Other authors have conducted more comprehensive

---

[4] The theological fallout of the controversy is discussed by Germain Grisez and the late John Ford, S.J., in "Contraception and the Infallibility of the Ordinary Magisterium," *Theological Studies* 39:2 (June 1978).

[5] John Finnis, *Natural Law and Natural Rights* (Oxford: Clarendon, 1980).

[6] Germain Grisez, "The First Principle of Practical Reason: A Commentary on *the Summa theologiae*, 1–2, Question 94, Article 2," *Natural Law Forum* (1965).

[7] See *In Defense of Natural Law* (New York: Clarendon, 1999).

[8] *Ethica Thomistica: The Moral Philosophy of Thomas Aquinas* (Washington, D.C.: Catholic University of America Press, 1982), and *Aquinas on Human Action: a Theory of Practice* (Washington, D.C.: Catholic University of America Press, 1992).

[9] *Swimming Against the Current in Contemporary Philosophy* (Washington, D.C.: Catholic University of America Press, 1990).

[10] *A Critique of the New Natural Law Theory* (Notre Dame: Notre Dame University Press, 1987).

[11] *Ethics in Context: Towards the Definition and Differentiation of the Morally Good* (London: Macmillan, and Washington, D.C.: Georgetown University Press, 1987).

historical surveys;[12] my intention in these first four chapters is to clarify the conceptual origins of natural law, to highlight major developments and transitions from ancient times to the present, to search for
some common features or patterns found in the various approaches,
and to indicate its present status as a theory. In Chapters 5 and 6 I try
to address the welter of challenges faced by anyone promoting natural law in the modern world—the changed view of nature; whether
natural-law theory is compromised as a philosophical approach by
dependence on a divine Legislator; whether major confusions of fact
and value, "is" and "ought," are inevitable with natural law; whether
any theory can measure up to the rigid Ciceronean standard of validity for all times and all places; and other problems. In Chapter 7 I pro-
pose what seems to me a solution of sorts to the plurality of interpretations—a differentiation of natural law in the strict sense, from
empirical natural law, and from a natural law analogous with scientific
laws; and I explore the possibilities for the latter analogical interpretations in considerable detail. Finally, in Chapter 8, since a theory presumably should be tested by its applicability, I consider what would be
a viable natural-law approach to some controversial contemporary
issues.

I would like to thank the Bradley Institute for Democracy and
Public Values for the initial funding which made possible exploratory
research leading to the writing of this book; and also my research
assistants Silas Langley, Ginger Lee, and Heather Ross, for help in
keeping up with the burgeoning literature on natural law.

---

[12] See, for example, Michael Crowe, *The Changing Profile of the Natural Law* (The
Hague: Nijhoff, 1977); and Pauline Westerman, *The Disintegration of Natural Law
Theory: Aquinas to Finnis* (Leiden: Brill, 1998).

1

Concepts of Natural Law in Ancient Greece and Rome

Natural law in the strict sense and as an explicit theory emerged, as we shall see, with the Stoics. But the evolution of the concept can be traced with fairly definite outlines through the pre-Socratics, Plato, and Aristotle, with some reverberations in Greek literature.

Pre-Socratic Developments

The Milesian philosopher **Anaximander** (610–547 B.C.) portrays nature itself as accomplishing moral purposes as it evolves, achieving "justice" (*diké*) by finally compensating for excesses or deficiencies in the operations of individual beings. In the cosmos as a whole everything eventually returns to its origins—but only after all beings have made "reparation and satisfaction to one another for their injustice according to the ordering of time."[1] The Ionian philosopher **Pythagoras** (570–500 B.C.) emphasized the mathematical or geometrical harmony existing in the cosmos, and theorized that through a process of purification the human soul could become a participant in this harmony.[2] **Heraclitus** (540–475 B.C.) developed the notion of *logos* as a tension of opposites in the universe, and speaks about a

---

[1] John Burnet, *Early Greek Philosophy* (Cleveland: World Publishing, 1963), 52.
[2] Iamblichus, *Life of Pythagoras*, trans. Thomas Taylor (London: Watkins, 1965), 5, 35ff, 81ff, 117.

1

single "divine law" by which "all the laws of men are nourished";[3] and Aristotle's principle of "right reason" (*orthos logos*, discussed below) seems to be an extension of this Heraclitean notion into the ethical domain, as maintaining an equilibrium between opposites.[4] The Athenian tragedian **Aeschylus** (525–456 B.C.) in his play, *Eumenides*, explores the just and natural punishments for the infraction of laws against matricide, homicide, and adultery; and the later Greek dramatist **Sophocles** (495–406 B.C.) in an even more explicit fashion focuses in *Oedipus the King* on the unnaturalness of incest and patricide, and in *Antigone* on the natural or divine law[5] of fidelity to family obligations. Sophocles posed the initial challenge of natural law very forcefully: Certainly if there are any acts which are so unnatural as to be loathsome and evil, the acts of incest and patricide (depicted in *Oedipus the King*) and the desecration of the corpse of one's sibling (depicted in *Antigone*) would be included in that list. The conflict between Antigone, refusing to forego the sacred burial rites for her brother, and King Creon, forbidding the burial rites for the "common good," became the classic *cause célèbre* exemplifying possible conflicts between natural law and human law. The frequent pre-Socratic conflation of nature and morality is found also in **Anaxagoras** (499–422 B.C.),who makes no distinction between human and non-human segments of the cosmos; everything exists in a quasi-moral relationship to everything else, incurring responsibility and indebtedness in mutual interactions.

The more "modern" concern about the difference between actually prevailing laws and certain laws which cannot be abrogated or changed by human authorities began to be recognized in the fifth century B.C. **Hippias** (ca. 460–390 B.C.) spoke about a divine law that

---

[3] G.S. Kirk and J.E. Raven, *The Presocratic Philosophers* (Cambridge: Cambridge University Press, 1957), Fragment 253.

[4] Aristotle, *Nicomachean Ethics,* trans. W.D. Ross, in Richard McKeon, ed., *The Basic Works of Aristotle* (New York: Random House, 1941) II, 1103b; VI, 1144b.

[5] In ancient philosophy, natural law is often referred to as "divine," in contrast with the merely human. In the medieval era, as we shall see in Chapter 2, the "divine law" is more closely connected with Revelation (the Judaeo-Christian tradition), and begins to be differentiated from natural law after some initial ambiguities. It should be noted that the notion of a purely "secular" natural law, discerned by the use of reason alone in a philosophical ethics and unrelated to theology, is an even later development, the origins of which are discussed below, in Chapter 3.

can never and nowhere be superseded, and under Socratic influence began to associate the divine or natural law with a universal abstract Form of Law.[6] But the task of fully developing what Socrates's pupil, **Xenophon** (ca. 430–355 B.C.) referred to as the contrast of an "unwritten law" (*agraphos nomos*) with human conventions, and connecting unwritten law with nature itself, *nomos* with *phusis*,[7] fell to the lot of later philosophers.

The Foreshadowing of Natural-Law Theory in Plato

We run into semantic problems when discussing natural law in **Plato**. The best-known distinction that Plato makes between the "law of nature" and conventional laws is *just the opposite* of natural-law theory—one might say, a perversion. In the *Gorgias*, Plato's Callicles, like a proto-Nietzschean, characterizes the "law of nature" as the law of superior people whom the majority try to keep in check with pedestrian laws:

> On what principle of justice did Xerxes invade Hellas, or his father the Scythians? (not to speak of numberless other examples). Nay, but these are the men who act according to nature; yes, by Heaven, and according to the law of nature: not, perhaps, according to that artificial law, which we invent and impose upon our fellows, of whom we take the best and strongest from their youth upwards, and tame them like young lions, — charming them with the sound of the voice, and saying to them, that with equality they must be content, and that the equal is the honourable and the just.[8]

Callicles here expresses his rejection of conventional laws as encumbrances, and refers to them pejoratively as "artificial." They do

---

[6] Rudolf Hirzel, *Agraphos Nomos* (Leipzig, 1900), 28–29.

[7] F.E. Peters, *Greek Philosophical Terms: A Historical Lexicon* (New York: New York University Press, 1967), 131.

[8] Plato, *Gorgias*, 483e, in *The Dialogues of Plato*, Benjamin Jowett trans. (New York: Random House, 1937). All the following Plato texts, unless otherwise noted, are from this edition.

not incorporate or reflect the "law of nature," but are antithetical to the "laws" that Xerxes *et al* are following.

In Plato's *Laws*, a similar position is attributed by the Athenian Stranger, to certain philosophers who invite people to live "according to nature":

> In the first place, my friend, these people would say that . . . the honourable is one thing by nature and another thing by law, and that the principles of justice have no existence at all in nature, but that mankind are always disputing about them and altering them; and that the alterations which are made by art [human creativity] and by law have no basis in nature, but are of authority for the moment and at the time at which they are made. These, my friends, are the sayings of wise men, poets and prose-writers, which find a way into the minds of youth. They are told by them that the highest right is might, and in this way the young fall into impieties.[9]

The Athenian Stranger concludes that this is the view consistent with the materialistic view that the soul arises out of material elements (earth, air, fire, water), rather than the opposite view that the soul comes first. In other words, "nature" in this context is something like the raw impulses that Freud associates with the Id, and a "law of nature" in this sense would be a pejoratively materialistic view of human relations.

But then the interlocutor of the Athenian Stranger, Cleinias, offers an indirect recognition of natural law, to which the Athenian Stranger offers qualified assent:

> *Cle.* [The legislator] ought to support the law and also art, and acknowledge that both alike exist by nature, and no less than nature, if they are creations of mind in accordance with right reason, as you appear to me to maintain, and I am disposed to agree with you in thinking.

> *Ath.* Yes, my enthusiastic Cleinias; but are not these things when spoken to the multitude hard to be understood, not to mention that they take up a dismal length of time?[10]

---

[9] Plato, *Laws*, X, 889e–890a.
[10] *Ibid.*, 890e.

Plato also offers approximations to the concept of natural law in the current sense, in the *Republic*,[11] in his analogy between health, as natural order in the body, and justice as the natural order of things in the state; and in his discussion of the formal idea of justice as "the just by nature" (*to phusei dikaion*);[12] and in the *Laws*, where the Athenian Stranger, discussing how to establish a state in which the law is above the rulers, proposes to speak to prospective colonists about a divine law which should supply the criterion for human justice:

> "Friends," we say to them, —"God, as the old tradition declares, holding in His hand the beginning, middle, and end of all that is, travels according to His nature in a straight line towards the accomplishment of His end. Justice always accompanies Him, and is the punisher of those who fall short of the divine law. To justice, he who would be happy holds fast, and follows in her company with all humility and order.[13]

This concept of an abstract, ideal, "divine" law existing prior to all human affairs bears a family resemblance to natural law. But while such indirect references in the *Republic* and *Laws* offer general adumbrations of some higher law, they fall short of an attempt to develop an explicit theory of natural law.

Natural Law and Natural Justice in Aristotle

Usually when one hears about the "Aristotelian roots" of natural law, reference is made to Aristotle's *Rhetoric*, where **Aristotle** refers to an unchanging, universal law. But in assessing the references in this text, we should keep in mind the fundamental point of view of the *Rhetoric*: It is like a handbook in the art of persuasion—the sort of things a lawyer *or* a prosecutor might study, in learning how best to make his case.

One of the first things on which a competent lawyer would focus, since "law" and "legality" tend to be amorphous umbrella terms,

---

[11] Plato, *Republic*, IV, 444e.
[12] *Ibid.*, V, 501b; *to phusei dikaion* is rendered "Absolute justice," in the Jowett translation.
[13] *Laws*, IV, 715e–716a.

would be to differentiate the various types of law and their ranges of applicability. Aristotle supplies the necessary distinctions at the outset: In the *Rhetoric* he distinguishes the kinds of persons subject to law— individuals and communities, and on this basis differentiates particular law from universal law. Particular law is then subdivided into written law (Aristotle offers the examples of laws against theft, mayhem, and adultery), and unwritten law (customs of approbation or disapprobation, or decisions of "equity" made by judges to compensate for the indeterminateness or overextension of legislative enactments). Then Aristotle discusses "universal" law, in a passage which is often cited as recognition and advocacy of natural law:

> Universal law is the law of Nature. For there really is, as every one to some extent divines, a natural justice and injustice that is binding on all men, even on those who have no association or covenant with each other. It is this that Sophocles' Antigone clearly means when she says that the burial of Polyneices was a just act in spite of the prohibition: she means that it was just by nature.
>
> *Not of to-day or yesterday it is,*
> *But lives eternal: none can date its birth.*
>
> And so Empedocles, when he bids us kill no living creature, says that doing this is not just for some people while unjust for others,
>
> *Nay, but, an all-embracing law, through the realms of the sky*
> *Unbroken it stretcheth, and over the earth's immensity.*
>
> And Alcidamas says in his Messeniac Oration
>
> *["God has left all men free; Nature has made no man slave"]*[14]

---

[14] Aristotle, *Rhetorica*, W. Rhys Roberts, trans., in McKeon, *Basic Works of Aristotle*, I,13, 1373b, 6–17. The speech of Antigone is found in Sophocles, *Antigone* 456:7. The passage from Empedocles in the Wheelwright translation reads, "What is lawful is not binding only on some and not binding on others. Lawfulness extends everywhere, through the wide-ruling air and the boundless light of the sky" (Philip Wheelwright, *The Presocratics* [New York: Odyssey Press, 1966], 142). Alcidamas of Elis was a pupil of Gorgias, and his comments refer to the revolt of the Messenians from Sparta. The elipsis in Aristotle's manuscript is supplied by the scholiast.

When Aristotle refers to a law which is "binding on all men," he seems to be going significantly beyond the concept of what in the Western tradition of political philosophy is called the "social contract." His citation of Sophocles, Empedocles, and Alcidamas could be taken as appeals to recognized authorities, to buttress his arguments asserting the existence of natural law. The reference to Sophocles's protagonist, Antigone, disobeying King Creon's prohibition of burial for her brother because of a higher law which commands reverence for kinfolk, seems *prima facie* to amount to a defense of natural law. But the reference to Empedocles is not so clear-cut.

Empedocles was a mystic and sage who preached vegetarianism, and even prohibited the eating of certain types of vegetables—for example, beans, in which reincarnated souls were thought to exist. Is Aristotle seriously arguing here, along with Empedocles, that we should be vegetarians? If so, it is strange that he intimates nothing like this in his ethical writings. Moreover, would Aristotle, who emphasized the unique relationship of the individual soul to a specific body,[15] give indirect support to Empedocles's theory of reincarnation? The doubts about Aristotle's intention in these passages become even more pronounced with regard to the citation of Alcidamas. Alcidamas's notion of freedom as the natural state runs directly counter to Aristotle's theory in the *Politics*[16] that there are "natural slaves" in the human race, and that it is best for such people to be under the control of a slave master.

In *Rhetoric* I, 15, 1374a, 26-31, it becomes clear that, although Aristotle himself may have believed in the existence of natural law, this is not the thrust of his arguments. Aristotle is *not* citing the example of Antigone and the other instances to argue for the existence or the validity of natural law, but rather as advice to a defense lawyer on how to win his case. He starts off with the viewpoint of the defense, in an adversary system:

> If the written law tells against our case, clearly we must appeal to the universal law, and insist on its greater equity and justice. We must argue that

---

[15] Aristotle, *De Anima,* J.A. Smith, trans., in McKeon, *Basic Works of Aristotle,* I, 3, 407b.
[16] Aristotle, *Politics,* trans. Benjamin Jowett, in McKeon, *Basic Works of Aristotle,* I, 2, 1252a; III, 14, 1285a.

the juror's oath "I will give my verdict according to honest opinion" means that one will not simply follow the letter of the written law.

Aristotle goes on to cite the passage from Sophocles's *Antigone* again, along with other ways of appealing to a universal law. *But then he follows up with advice for the prosecutor:*

> If however the written law supports our case, we must urge that the oath "to give my verdict according to my honest opinion" is not meant to make the judges give a verdict that is contrary to the law, but to save them from the guilt of perjury if they misunderstand what the law really means. Or that no one chooses what is absolutely good, but every one what is good for himself. Or that not to use the laws is as bad as to have no laws at all. Or that, as in the other arts, it does not pay to try to be cleverer than the doctor: for less harm comes from the doctor's mistakes than from the growing habit of disobeying authority. Or that trying to be cleverer than the laws is just what is forbidden by those codes of law that are accounted best.

Here Aristotle is offering pointers particularly to prosecutors or judges who are faced with arguments appealing to "eternal laws" or exceptional cases which may invite "equity" decisions or "judicial reviews" which reinterpret or modify the laws. He would have to be a cynic or extreme relativist to make such statements in a strictly normative manner.

In his *Nicomachean Ethics* V, 7, 1134b18-1135a4, however, Aristotle does make observations about "natural justice" which approximate to the concept of natural law, but should not be confused with natural-law theory in the strict sense:

> Of political justice part is natural, part legal, —natural, that which everywhere has the same force and does not exist by people's thinking this or that; legal, that which is originally indifferent, but when it has been laid down is not indifferent, e.g. that a prisoner's ransom shall be a mina, or that a goat and not two sheep shall be sacrificed, and again all the laws that are passed for particular cases. . . . Now some think that all justice is of this sort, because that which is by nature is unchangeable and has everywhere the same force (as fire burns both here and in Persia), while they see change in the things recognized as just. This, however, is not true in this unqualified way. . . . With us there is something that is just even by nature, yet all of it is changeable; but still some is by nature, some not by nature.

. . . By nature the right hand is stronger, yet it is possible that all men should come to be ambidextrous. The things which are just by virtue of convention and expediency are like measures; for wine and corn measures are not everywhere equal, but large in wholesale and smaller in retail markets. Similarly, the things which are just not by nature but by human enactment are not everywhere the same, since constitutions also are not the same, though there is but one which is everywhere by nature the best.

Conspicuously absent from this analysis of natural justice are norms such as those mentioned above from the *Rhetoric*—duties to kinfolk, as exemplified by Antigone, respect for life, as inculcated by Empedocles, or the natural human freedom theorized by Alcidamas. In interpreting this passage, we should keep in mind that for Aristotle, ethics is a branch of politics, and that the context for this discussion is an analysis of the virtue of justice—not justice in the global sense of "virtuousness" or "righteousness" but with regard to the responsible interchange of goods in political society. The references to "wine and corn measures" and to the standards of justice in various political constitutions emphasize the context of commutative and distributive justice, and also rectificatory justice, as the example of prisoner's bail-charges indicates. The reference to right-handedness is meant to show that general rules of justice, unlike the burning characteristics of fire, admit of exceptions. Aquinas in his commentary on Aristotle's *Nichomachean Ethics* offers as an example the rule of natural justice about returning a person's property to them, which is for the most part valid, but admits exceptions:

> Those actions that follow (from the nature of justice) are changeable in a few cases. For example, nothing seems to be more just than that a deposit should be returned to the owner. Nevertheless the return must not be made to a madman demanding his sword or to a traitor to his country demanding money for arms.[17]

In short, "natural justice" in the context of Aristotle's ethics consists of general rules for the distribution, exchange, or transmission of goods, based on the economic exigencies of human society.

---

[17] *In decem libros Ethicorum Aristotelis ad Nicomachum expositio* Thomae Aquinatis, cura et studio Raymundi M.Spiazzi (Taurini: Marietti, 1949), Vol. I, Bk 5, lec 12, 439ff, §§1023, 1029, 1025; Aquinas uses the same example in his discussion of "secondary precepts" of the natural law in *Summa theologiae*, 1ª2ᵃᵉ q. 94, a. 4c.

Finally, it is conceivable that natural human sociability itself constitutes a significant element of a latent natural-law theory in Aristotle. For example, his emphasis in the *Politics* on the fact that humans are essentially political animals, and that the state is thus a creation of nature itself, might be arguably interpreted as a natural law of forming and participating in cities and states. But explicitly Aristotle neither enunciates nor expands on any natural-law theory in the traditional sense.[18]

Stoic Natural Law

Ancient Greek Stoics such as Zeno of Citium (335–264 B.C.) and Chrysippus (280–206 B.C.) focused primarily on logic, epistemology, metaphysics, and ethics. The few fragments of their ethical writings which are extant emphasize living according to nature, but the further development of this idea was the work of Roman stoics.

Marcus Tullius **Cicero** (106–43 B.C.), admitting that he borrowed heavily from the Greeks,[19] and that his ideas were not particularly original, nevertheless was responsible for the most systematic development of the concept of natural law into an explicit ethical theory. His famous definition of natural law in *On the Republic*, helps to sum up the intent and general thrust, if not the content, of all later natural-law theories, bringing out its universality and timelessness, the inseparability of rationality and nature, and its divine origin:

> True law is right reason conformable to nature, universal, unchangeable, eternal, whose commands urge us to duty, and whose prohibitions restrain us from evil. Whether it enjoins or forbids, the good respect its injunctions, and the wicked treat them with indifference. This law cannot be contradicted by any other law, and is not liable either to derogation or abrogation. Neither the senate nor the people can give us any dispensation for not obeying this universal law of justice. It needs no other expositor and interpreter than our own conscience. It is not one thing at Rome,

---

[18] Aristotle, *Politics*, I, 2, 1253a, 1–9.
[19] Cicero in 97 B.C. traveled to Rhodes to consult with Posidonius (135–50 B.C.). In *De officiis*, Cicero says that he is largely aligned with the doctrines of Panaetius (180–110 B.C.). He cites Chrysippus frequently in *De finibus*.

and another at Athens; one thing today and another to-morrow, but in all times and nations this universal law must for ever reign, eternal and imperishable. It is the sovereign master and emperor of all beings. God himself is its author, its promulgator, its enforcer. And he who does not obey it flies from himself, and does violence to the very nature of man. And by so doing he will endure the severest penalties even if he avoid the other evils which are usually accounted punishments.[20]

The contrast between natural law and prevailing positive laws could not be brought out more clearly. Natural law is characterized as above all national laws and constitutions. Since it "cannot be contradicted" it can invalidate positive laws, making them null and void (although the issue of whether such invalid laws can or should still be obeyed is left open). The idealization of natural law as the "sovereign master and emperor" finds its parallel in the democratic ideal that even the leader (at least in theory) is subject to the sovereign rule of law.

In *On the Laws*, Cicero portrays natural law as a potent instrument for reform, if not for "civil disobedience" or even revolution:

If the will of the people, the decrees of the senate, the adjudications of magistrates, were sufficient to establish rights, then it might become right to rob, right to commit adultery, right to substitute forged wills, if such conduct were sanctioned by the votes or decrees of the multitude. . . . Are the laws of tyrants just, simply because they are laws? Suppose the thirty tyrants of Athens had imposed certain laws on the Athenians? or, suppose again that these Athenians were delighted with these tyrannical laws, would these laws on that account have been considered just?[21]

But if natural law is really, and not just metaphorically or by analogy, a *law*, a lawgiver is implied. In the dialogue between Marcus and Quintus in *On the Laws*, Marcus, expressing Cicero's point of view, and the position of many later natural-law theorists, traces natural law to God as the supreme lawgiver, or more specifically to the mind or reason of God:

---

[20] Marcus Tullius Cicero, *On the Republic*, Charles Duke Yonge, trans. (London: H.G. Bohn, 1853), III, 22.

[21] Cicero, *On the Laws*, Charles Duke Yonge trans. (London: H.G. Bohn, 1853), I, 12, 18.

This, then, as it appears to me, has been the decision of the wisest philosophers, that law was neither a thing contrived by the genius of man, nor established by any decree of the people, but a certain eternal principle, which governs the entire universe, wisely commanding what is right and prohibiting what is wrong. Therefore they called that aboriginal and supreme law the mind of God, enjoining or forbidding each separate thing in accordance with reason. [The power of law] is not only far more ancient than any existence of states and peoples, but is coeval with God himself, who beholds and governs both heaven and earth.[22]

In the writings of the later Roman Stoics the appeal to a higher, divine or natural law superseding all civil laws is continued, and two additional themes are recurrent and common:

1. *The emphasis on world citizenship and equality:* What proponents of world unity would now consider the "progressive" Stoic emphasis on human equality was conditioned by the political, legal, and geographical aspects of Rome as it expanded from a Republic to a worldwide empire. As the empire extended through war and politics into Asia, the Middle East, Europe, and Africa, cosmopolitan Roman citizenship, with its rights and privileges, as well as its responsibilities, instilled a sense of unity transcending local and national allegiances.

The freed slave and Stoic **Epictetus** (60–138 A.D.), gave philosophical expression to the new value system which was emerging in tandem with the new political realities: "Never, when asked one's country, [should you answer], "I am an Athenian or a Corinthian," but "I am a citizen of the world."[23]

2. *An emphasis on coordination with the cycles of nature:* It is difficult for us in the twenty-first century to identify with ancient Roman cosmology. Contemporary science emphasizes a linear evolutionary progression through an expanding universe arriving through explosions and cataclysms at complex sidereal and planetary systems, leading eventually to life on our particular planet through Darwinian struggles for survival of the fittest. The cosmology prevailing in the

---

[22] *Ibid.*, I, 2, 4–5.
[23] Epictetus, *The Golden Sayings of Epictetus*, Hastings Crossley trans., Vol. II, Part 2, in The Harvard Classics (New York: Collier, 1909–1914), #15.

era of Stoicism, in sharp contrast, was cyclical in nature—the fixed stars pursuing their appointed courses, the sun and moon presiding over recurrent and largely predictable seasonal changes, with which persons must coordinate their lives.

In the writings of the Stoic emperor **Marcus Aurelius** (121–180 A.D.) this is a continuing theme:

> All that is from the gods is full of Providence. That which is from fortune is not separated from nature or without an interweaving and involution with the things which are ordered by Providence. From thence all things flow; and there is besides necessity, and that which is for the advantage of the whole universe, of which thou art a part. But that is good for every part of nature which the nature of the whole brings, and what serves to maintain this nature. . . . Everything harmonizes with me, which is harmonious to thee, O Universe. Nothing for me is too early nor too late, which is in due time for thee. Everything is fruit to me which thy seasons bring, O Nature: from thee are all things, in thee are all things, to thee all things return.[24]

Thus we find in Stoic natural-law theory very general but ground-breaking concepts of divine governance, of rationality or *logos* embedded in nature, universal human equality and brotherhood, and the ideal of respecting and harmonizing oneself with nature. Medieval natural-law theory will continue this emphasis on timeless and divinely inculcated laws, and coordination with nature—but largely within an Aristotelian framework.

---

[24] *The Meditations of Marcus Aurelius Antonius,* George Long trans. (Mount Vernon: Peter Pauper Press, 195??), II, IV.

2

Aquinas and Suarez

Prior Developments in Roman Jurisprudence

The Stoic concept of a universal law became more refined and nuanced at the hands of later Roman jurists. **Gaius** (130–180 A.D.) identified the natural law (*jus naturale*)[1] with the "law of nations" (*jus gentium*), the latter being defined as the rational element underlying all judicial systems, not some ideal standard associated with Stoicism. With **Ulpian** (170–228) a distinction was made between the two *jura*—*jus naturale* being defined more broadly than *jus gentium*, as what is taught by nature to all animals (not just humans). Under this rubric, the natural freedom of human beings was justified as a natural-law issue, while slavery was ascribed to the "law of nations," as empirically supported in the legal codes of many nations. Various edicts by Emperors Claudius, Vespasian, and Antoninus, freeing slaves in certain circumstances in the first and second century, exemplify the tension in emerging Roman law between the natural law of freedom and the licit slavery countenanced by the *jus gentium*.

The East Roman Christian Emperor **Justinian** (483–565) provided an important impetus to natural-law thinking by overseeing a codification of the laws. He developed the *Corpus Juris Civilis* (initial compilation completed in A.D. 534), consisting of three parts: the

---

[1] The Latin *jus*, like the German *Recht*, can mean either "law" or "right," depending on the context. Sometimes both meanings are intended in early medieval philosophy.

Digest of writings from earlier jurists, the *Institutes* or elementary instructions for schools, and the *Codex* (Codification) of the Imperial Constitution. In the *Digest*, a distinction between *jus civile, jus gentium*, and *jus naturale* was made, often with conflicting definitions offered by Ulpian, Gaius, and other authors excerpted in the *Digest*. The *Institutes* led in a rather different direction: They not only distinguished *natural law* from *jus gentium*, but portrayed natural law as a set of immutable divine laws which could be used in judging the validity of civil laws.

The main element that caught the attention of later jurists and philosophers was the idea of a universal law, after the Stoic model, distinct from civil laws, and providing criteria for evaluating the latter. But it should be noted that among the Romans natural law did not supersede or invalidate civil law, while for later thinkers positive law could be revoked on behalf of natural law, setting the stage for such events as the American and French revolutions.

The Benedictine monk **Gratian** (ca. 1100–1159) produced the *Decretum Gratiani,* a compilation of thousands of texts resulting from previous church councils. The *Decretum*, included in what later came to be called the *Corpus juris canonici*, rose to an importance equal to the *Corpus juris civilis* of Justinian. In the *Decretum*, the idea of natural law is given a distinctively theological connotation: "Mankind is ruled by two laws: Natural Law and Custom. Natural Law is that which is contained in the Law and the Gospel." In other words, although the divine law in the Scriptures goes beyond morality, it contains some immutable moral directives; Gratian offers the example of the "Golden Rule," from the Gospels [2] and from the Old Testament,[3] and "thou shalt not kill" from the Decalogue.[4] Gratian, in emphasizing that the natural law is fundamental to the divine law, is echoing the position of St. Isidore of Seville (560–636): "All laws are either divine or human. Divine laws are based on nature, human laws on custom."

Thus a variety of definitions of natural law—either as a subset of the divine law, or some specific Scriptural injunctions, or some common international values, or inclinations possessed by humans in

---

[2] *Matthew* 7:12; *Luke* 6:31.
[3] *Tobit* 4:15.
[4] *Exodus* 20:2–17; *Deuteronomy* 5:6–21.

common with animals—prevailed by the time that Thomas Aquinas set himself to clarify and apply natural law in the thirteenth century.

Thomas Aquinas and Natural-Law Theory

The approach to natural law of St. Thomas **Aquinas** (1225–1274) is as an integral part of a systematic analysis of the nature and types of law, and is distinguished by its synthesis of Aristotelian philosophy and Christian theology, as well as by an incorporation of critical analysis of prevailing legal traditions. Aquinas makes an important distinction between the "divine" law set forth in the Scriptures and the "eternal" law governing the universe, and portrays natural law as the participation of the Eternal law by rational creatures.[5] In other words, the eternal law takes precedence, and gives rise to the natural law; the divine law revealed in the Scriptures reiterates aspects of the natural law, along with sacred history, ritual and mystical directives, counsels of perfection, and so forth; and civil law, at its best, will incorporate much of the natural law that pertains to social order. Aquinas incorporates Ulpian's comment that natural law is "that which nature has taught all animals," but goes beyond this to recognize ontological inclinations and specifically rational inclinations.[6] He carries the distinction between human law and natural law to its logical conclusion, maintaining that all human laws must conform to natural law in order to be valid.[7] But while Gratian had categorized private property and slavery as developments in the *jus gentium*, Aquinas portrays them rather as developments which add to, but do not necessarily subtract from, the natural law.[8]

Vernon Bourke's doubts about whether Aquinas can be called a natural-law ethicist[9] result largely from the fact that Aquinas is much

---

[5] *Summa theologica*, 1ᵃ 2ᵃᵉ, q. 91, arts. 1–2., 996. The present text and all of the following texts are from the first part of *St. Thomas Aquinas, Summa Theologica, Part II*, in the first complete American Edition in three volumes, literally translated by Fathers of the English Dominican Province, Vol. I, published by Benziger Brothers, Inc., 1947. Hereafter, this edition is abbreviated as *ST*.

[6] *ST*, 1ᵃ2ᵃᵉ, q.94, a.2., 1009.

[7] *ST*, 1ᵃ2ᵃᵉ, q.95, a.2, 1014.

[8] *ST*, 1ᵃ2ᵃᵉ, q.94, a.5, 1012.

[9] "Is Thomas Aquinas a Natural Law Ethicist?" *The Monist* (1974), 6.

more than that. His discussions of natural law are imbedded in sections which incorporate discussions of ethical and legal principles, virtues, moral theology, and so forth; and, as Bourke observes, Aquinas's early emphasis on "natural inclinations" is more nuanced in his later works. Also, Aquinas's attempts to defend the principle of the coordination of nature and grace continually place natural law in a theological framework.

The main section of the *Summa* where Aquinas gives specific attention to natural law is in 1ª2ᵃᵉ, Q. 94, although discussion of natural law is interspersed through many other sections. In Q. 94, Aquinas begins by clarifying the relationship of natural law to law in general:

> The rule and measure of human acts is reason, which is the first principle of human acts. . . . It belongs to reason to direct to the end, which is the first principle in all matters of action. . . . Reason has its power of moving from the will. . . . for it is due to the fact that one wills the end, that reason issues its commands as regards things ordained to the end.[10]

In matters of practical reasoning, the last is first, so to speak. The goal or end must be conceptualized before any actions can be elicited. Law of any kind is goal-oriented. If there is such a thing as natural law, it would have to be based on the ends of nature. The presupposition, of course, is that nature is teleological; and Aquinas follows Aristotle[11] in contending that we can discover teleologies in all natural beings and that the teleology of human beings is the pursuit of happiness. Law, then, is related to happiness, but not merely individual happiness. A simple command might have to do with individual happiness, but law is intrinsically social or communal:

> The last end of human life is bliss or happiness, as stated above. Consequently the law must needs regard principally the relationship to happiness. Moreover, since every part is ordained to the whole as imperfect to perfect; and since one man is a part of the perfect community, the law must needs regard properly the relationship to universal happiness.[12]

---

[10] *ST*, 1ª2ᵃᵉ, q.90, a.1, 993–94.
[11] See especially the first book of the *Nicomachean Ethics*.
[12] *ST*, 1ª2ᵃᵉ q.90, a.2, 994.

Modern theorizing about community, in the aftermath of Hobbes and Locke, tends to start with the monadic individual and work up analytically to sociopolitical constructions. In the Thomistic or Aristotelian political philosophy, the analysis takes place in the other direction. Humans are naturally social beings, and cannot be understood or flourish except in connection with family, community, and polity—the whole, of which they form constituent and indispensable parts.

Natural law is analogous to human law, in which a legislator "can impose laws on rational beings subject to him, in so far as, by his command or pronouncement, he imprints on their minds a rule which is a principle of action."[13] God as legislator acts in a similar way:

> Since all things subject to Divine providence are ruled and measured by the eternal law, . . . it is evident that all things partake somewhat of the eternal law, in so far as, namely, from its being impressed on them, they derive their respective inclinations to their proper acts and ends. Now among all others, the rational creature is subject to Divine providence in the most excellent way, in so far as it partakes of a share of providence, by being provident both for itself and for others. Wherefore it has a share of the Eternal Reason, whereby it has a natural inclination to its proper act and end: and this participation of the eternal law in the rational creature is called the natural law.[14]

In the above two passages, Aquinas says the human legislator "imprints" (*imprimit*) a rule on the mind, and that human inclinations result from an "impression" (*impressione*) of the eternal law on human nature. The language here is somewhat Platonic, possibly *via* Augustinian influence. The idea seems to be that what we experience as fundamental human inclinations are aspects of the eternal law instilled into human nature, orienting humans toward certain natural goals. Human beings have a natural inclination to accomplish the general ends congruent with their nature, and this inclination is a mark or impression of the eternal law in which they are participating. Natural law thus is the actual participation in the eternal law, facilitated by human inclinations to implement the will of the divine legis-

---

[13] *ST*, 1ª2ᵃᵉ q.93, a.5, 1006.
[14] *ST*, 1ª2ᵃᵉ q.91, a.2, 997.

lator. These natural inclinations lead humans to cooperate in divine providence, even though they may not be aware that they are doing so.

The primordial springboard for human participation in the eternal law is the fundamental rational apprehension that "good is to be done and pursued, and evil is to be avoided." This is the "first precept" of the natural law.[15] "The good" for humans is happiness, but the very general orientation towards this good can be more specifically defined or clarified in terms of the natural inclinations essentially associated with human nature, thus leading to three pivotal secondary precepts:

> The order of the precepts of the natural law exists according to the order of natural inclinations. Because in man there is first of all an inclination to good in accordance with the nature which he has in common with all substances: inasmuch as every substance seeks the preservation of its own being, according to its nature: and by reason of this inclination, whatever is a means of preserving human life, and of warding off its obstacles, belongs to the natural law. Secondly, there is in man an inclination to things that pertain to him more specially, according to that nature which he has in common with other animals: and in virtue of this inclination, those things are said to belong to the natural law, which nature has taught to all animals, such as sexual intercourse, education of offspring and so forth. Thirdly, there is in man an inclination to good, according to the nature of his reason, which nature is proper to him: thus man has a natural inclination to know the truth about God, and to live in society: and in this respect, whatever pertains to this inclination belongs to the natural law; for instance, to shun ignorance, to avoid offending those among whom one has to live, and other such things regarding the above inclination."[16]

---

[15] *ST*, 1ª2ae q.94, a.2, 1009.

[16] *ST*, 1ª2ae q.94, a.2, 1009–1010: *Quia vero bonum habet rationem finis, malum autem rationem contrarii, inde est, quod omnia illa ad quae homo habet naturalem inclinationem, ratio naturaliter apprehendit ut bona, et per consequens ut opere prosequenda, et contraria eorum ut mala et vitanda. Secundum igitur ordinem inclinationum naturalium, est ordo praeceptorum legis naturae. Inest enim primo inclinatio homini ad bonum secundum naturam in qua communicat cum omnibus substantiis: prout scilicet quaelibet substantia appetit conservationem sui esse secundum suam naturam. Et secundum hanc inclinationem pertinent ad legem naturalem ea per quae vita hominis conservatur, et contrarium impeditur. —Secundo inest homini inclinatio ad aliqua magis specialia, secundum naturam in qua communicat cum ceteris animalibus.*

This is a crucial text, subject to disparate interpretations by contemporary natural law theorists. What seems uncontroversial in this passage is that Aquinas gets beyond "do good and avoid evil," and gets more specific about the precepts of the natural law. When he talks about what human nature "has in common with all substances," he is echoing the Aristotelian notion that natural beings—even rocks and water-lilies—have an "appetite" for existing and preserving themselves in existence. The other two references, to the inclinations in common with animals and to the specific rational inclinations, are consonant with Aristotelian philosophical anthropology,[17] according to which the "specific difference" of the human soul is rationality, but the rational soul contains the animal or sensitive soul "virtually."

This trifold division is not original with Aquinas. The first two divisions are clearly distinguished by Cicero, who writes,

> The first thing to be taken notice of is this, that every creature doth by nature endeavour to preserve its own self, its life and body; and to shun and avoid those things which appear prejudicial and hurtful to it; but to seek and procure whatever is necessary for the support of its being, and advancement of its happiness, such as food, shelter, and the like. There is likewise common to all sorts of animals a desire for the continuance and propagation of their several species; together with a love and concern for their young ones.[18]

These two divisions, capped with a third division of a specifically "rational" inclination, are continued in medieval natural-law discussions by Aquinas's predecessors and contemporaries. **William of Auxerre** (ca. 1150–1231) discerns three levels of natural laws, corresponding to three levels of commonality in nature: *jus naturale*

Et secundum hoc, dicuntur ea esse de lege natural quae natura omnia animalia docuit, ut est coniunctio maris et feminae, et educatio liberorum, et similia. —Tertio modo inest homini inclinatio ad bonum secundum naturam rationis, quae est sibi propria: sicut homo habet naturalem inclinationem ad hoc quod veritatem cognoscat de Deo, et ad hoc quod in societate vivat. Et secundum hoc, ad legem naturalem pertinent ea quae ad huiusmodi inclinationem spectant: utpote quod homo ignorantiam vitet, quod alios non offendat cum quibus debet conversari, et cetera huiusmodi quae ad hoc spectant.

[17] See especially Aristotle's *De anima*, in which the theory of the tripartite living-sensing-reasoning human soul is developed.

[18] Cicero, *De Officiis*, I:4, p. 13.

speciale, found only in rational beings; *jus naturale universalius*, found throughout animal nature; and *jus naturale universalissimum*, found in all creation, including inanimate creation.[19] **Roland of Cremona** and **Hugh of St. Cher**, holding chairs of theology at Paris in 1229–1230 and 1230–1235, respectively, follow William in their natural-law doctrines.

Aquinas correlates these divisions with the Aristotelian levels of being, and also attempts to show continuity with Roman law. His reference to what humans have "in common with other animals" is indebted to Gratian's definition, and Gratian's application to "the union of man and woman, the succession of children, the education of boys."[20] But the most important inclination of the triad is the inclination specific to humans—namely, the rational tendency,[21] naturally oriented towards knowledge and social life.

The three relevant precepts of natural law thus become: the precepts of self-preservation; parental responsibility for rearing and educating offspring; and the pursuit of knowledge and sociability (this might be interpreted minimally as social consciousness, maximally as love). It is interesting that Charles de Secondat **Montesquieu** (1689–1775), probably not influenced by Aquinas or the scholastic tradition, describes the basic inclinations of the "law of nature" along the same lines as Aquinas: towards "the preservation of his being" and "to seek for nourishment," toward "the attraction arising from the difference of sexes," and toward the "advantage of acquired knowledge" and the "desire of living in society." [22]

What is disputed in regard to this passage is whether Aquinas is actually "deriving" moral laws from natural inclinations—thus falling into the "naturalistic" fallacy. This issue will be discussed later in Chapter 6 of this book. For our present purposes, it should be noted that, in the Thomistic framework, if any deductions are made from

---

[19] Guillermo of Auxerre, *Summa Aurea in quattuor libros sententiarum* (Frankfurt am Main: Minerva GmbH, 1964), 153rb.

[20] Stanley Cunningham, "Albertus Magnus on Natural Law," *Journal of the History of Ideas* 28 (October–December 1967), 497; Cunningham cites Albertus Magnus, *De bono*, V, 1, 3, 271–72.

[21] *ST*, 1a2ae, q.94, a.4, 1011

[22] Charles Montesquieu, *The Spirit of the Laws*, Thomas Nugent translation (London: Bell, 1878), Book I, Chapter 2.

natural-law principles, they are not made with the sort of necessity that is possible in theoretical deductions from first principles. The general principle is that they apply "for the most part," but admit of exceptions. Aquinas emphasizes this lack of absoluteness, when he reflects on the characteristics of the conclusions of practical reason, as contrasted with the exceptionless conclusions of speculative reason:

> As to the proper conclusions of the speculative reason, the truth is the same for all, but is not equally known to all: thus it is true for all that the three angles of a triangle are together equal to two right angles, although it is not known to all. But as to the proper conclusions of the practical reason neither is the truth or rectitude the same for all, nor where it is the same, is it equally known by all. Thus it is right and true for all to act according to reason: and from this principle it follows as a proper conclusion, that goods entrusted to another should be restored to their owner. Now this is true for the majority of cases: but it may happen in a particular case that it would be injurious.[23]

> Nothing seems to be more just than that a deposit should be returned to the owner. Nevertheless the return must not be made to a madman demanding his sword or to a traitor to his country demanding money for arms.[24]

The emphasis on validity "for the most part" is also found in the relationship of natural law to actual civil and criminal laws. Natural law can be utilized effectively as a reliable standard for evaluating, and a source for deriving, such laws, as long as it does not try to descend into all the minute determinations (*determinationes*) inseparably connected with human lawmaking:

> Every human law has just so much of the nature of law, as it is derived from the law of nature. But if in any point it deflects from the law of nature, it is no longer a law but a perversion of law.
> But it must be noted that something may be derived from the natural law in two ways: first, as a conclusion from premises, secondly, by way of determination of certain generalities. The first way is like to that by

---

[23] *ST*, 1ª2ᵃᵉ, q.94, a.4, 1011.
[24] Thomas Aquinas, *Commentary on Aristotle's Nicomachean Ethics*, translated by C.I. Litzinger (Chicago: Regnery, 1964), #1025.

which, in sciences, demonstrated conclusions are drawn from the principles: while the second mode is likened to that whereby, in the arts, general forms are particularized as to details: thus the craftsman needs to
determine the general form of a house to some particular shape. Some
things are therefore derived from the general principles of the natural law,
by way of conclusions; e.g., that one must not kill may be derived as a
conclusion from the principle that one should do harm to no man: while
some are derived therefrom by way of determination; e.g., the law of
nature has it that the evil-doer should be punished; but that he be punished in this or that way, is a determination of the law of nature.
Accordingly both modes of derivation are found in the human law. But
those things which are derived in the first way, are contained in human
law not as emanating therefrom exclusively, but have some force from the
natural law also. But those things which are derived in the second way,
have no other force than that of human law.[25]

Although Aquinas does not consider the possibility that "perversions" of natural law through human laws might justify revolution,
one can discern potentially revolutionary implications, if the principle
that natural law validates or invalidates civil laws is applied to the
political order. For example, if the major premise of a natural-law
inference is that "taxation without representation is unjust," and the
minor premise is "that which is not just is no law at all," the conclusion of American revolutionaries that "taxation without representation is tyranny" would follow logically.

The table on the facing page indicates the hierarchy of some basic
natural-law directives in Aquinas's formulation.

In the last analysis, natural law for Aquinas is a dynamic mediating
factor, which helps maintain a harmonious relationship between
divine law on the one hand, and human law on the other:

Human law . . . is both something ordained to an end, and is a rule or
measure ruled or measured by a higher measure. And this higher measure
is twofold, viz., the Divine law and the natural law, as explained above.[26]

Human law is a "measure" for human activity, but is itself subject
to supervening measures. These "higher measures" consist not only

---

[25] *ST*, 1ª2ᵃᵉ q.95, a.3.
[26] *Ibid.*

General Principle of Practical Reason:	Good is to be pursued, and evil avoided
Secondary Precepts	Preserve your life; nurture and educate your children; pursue the truth and avoid causing any harm to others.
Examples of derivation of conclusions from secondary precepts (these possess some force from Natural Law)	Do not kill; help maintain social order; restore goods entrusted to you.
Examples of giving determination to certain generalities (these possess force only from human law)	Prison sentences, fines, and so forth, as a determination of the principle that evildoers should be punished.

of Divine law—for instance that the polity should be "compatible with religion" (*religioni congruat*)—but also with those basic precepts of natural law which can be rather directly connected with the self-evident principle of orientation toward the good.[27] The final determinate measurements of contingencies and special cases, however, are relegated to the civil authorities.

Suarez and Late Scholasticism

In the aftermath of the Protestant Reformation, and due in part to the reaction of Luther and other reformers to scholastic or Thomistic philosophy, development of natural-law theory was primarily the province of Catholic thinkers.

Francisco **Suarez** (1548–1617), the last of the great scholastics, like Aquinas developed a massive philosophical and theological system, although not in the identifiably Thomistic tradition. For example, Suarez broke rank with Aquinas on certain metaphysical issues, criticizing Aquinas's proof for God's existence from motion,

---

[27] *Ibid.*

and the Thomistic doctrine on the real distinction between essence and existence. Suarez has sometimes been characterized as a "voluntarist" in natural law—emphasizing the will of God rather than objective grounds in human nature, so that theoretically any kind of content could be a natural-law command. But this is to confuse Suarez with John Duns Scotus (1266–1308) and William of Ockham (1290–1349), who emphasized voluntarism in ethics. Suarez himself describes his approach as a "middle course" between voluntarism and intellectualism, and characterizes natural law as judgments concerning what is or is not in accord with human nature.[28] In his treatise on natural law, Suarez's analysis is even more systematic than that of Aquinas, and he goes into more detail in differentiating clear applications of natural law from questionable or merely probable applications.

Like Aquinas, Suarez emphasizes the connection of the natural law with the Divine/eternal law. It is made known to us in a twofold way, "first through natural reason, and secondly, through the law of the Decalogue written on the Mosaic tablets." [28] Suarez refers to St. Paul's admonition in *Romans* 2:14–15, accompanied by examples from the last seven commandments of the Decalogue, that the law of God is written on the hearts of all men. But if we would look for *empirical* confirmation of the rational application of the natural law, Suarez suggests that the "law of nations" is the closest approximation to it.

Clear applications of the natural law include "the commands relating to the restitution of the property of another, or the return of a deposit, or observing good faith in telling the truth," as well as in "the obligation to observe [treaties of peace and truces] after they are made."[30] But there is also a group of applications which fall short of clarity, and require considerable reflection.

In Book II of his *Treatise*,[31] Suarez discusses the hierarchy of applications of natural law, starting with the more obvious principles and derivations:

---

[28] Francisco Suarez, *A Treatise on Laws and God the Lawgiver*, in James Brown Scott, ed., *Selections from Three Works by Francisco Suarez*, Vol. II, (Oxford: Clarendon, 1944), II, v, §9, 183.
[29] Suarez, II, Introduction, 143.
[30] Suarez, II, xix, §9, 348.
[31] Suarez, II, 7, §5.

Primary and general principles of morality (clearly pertain to the natural law)	Examples: "one must do good, and shun evil," and the Golden Rule: "Do not to another that which you would not wish done to yourself."
Self-evident truths (the "law" amounts to a definition of terms)	Examples: "Justice must be observed"; "God must be worshiped"; "One must live temperately"—which involve analytic definitions of "justice," "God," and "living."
Conclusions which are deduced from natural principles by an evident inference, and which cannot become known save through rational reflection. **a) Those which are recognized more easily than others, and by a greater number of persons;**	Examples: Prohibitions against adultery and theft. In II, 7, §6 he adds: prohibitions "against simple fornication, usury, and vengeance inflicted upon an enemy by one's own authority"; and "affirmative commands to keep vows and promises, to give alms out of one's superfluous possessions, to honor one's parents."
b) those which require more reflection, of a sort not easily within the capacity of all; there may be only a dim consciousness of the seriousness of these infractions in many persons;	Examples: Intrinsic evil of fornication, the injustice of usury, the absolute prohibition of lying.
The *jus gentium*, law of nations, which can mean either 1) the law(s) regulating the relations of nations among one another, or 2) bodies of law within individual states that are comparable to laws in other states.	Examples: 1) Free trade among peaceful nations; respect for ambassadors, observance of just-war principles, acceptance of reasonable treaties and truces; 2) slavery as a punishment meted out by a nation victorious in a war against an aggressor nation.

As mentioned above,[32] *jus* in early medieval philosophy sometimes connoted both "law" and "right" or "justice"; the idea of
"rights" was also implicit in *jus*, in the sense that the property or
services that were the subject-matter of justice were considered
things to which one might have a right. But, as Heinrich Rommen
observes,[33] Suarez made a clear distinction between the usage of "*lex
naturalis*" ("law of nature") and "*ius naturale*," when he declared
that violation of the *lex naturalis* (e.g. divergent sexual mores) did
not constitute grounds for war with the American Indians. Only an
offense against the *ius naturale* (such as breaking a treaty) warrants
such action. Suarez also can also be said to have opened up the issue
of individual rights, insofar as he distinguishes *jus* in the general sense
and *jus* as an individual right over property, and so forth.[34]

The American experience in the sixteenth century was the catalyst
for a number of similar seminal discussions of "natural rights" or
"human rights." The Spanish Dominicans, Francisco de **Vitoria**
(1492–1546) and Bartolomé **de las Casas** (1474–1566), reflecting
critically on the Spanish conquest of the New World, insisted that natural rights inhered in humans and were being subverted by European
colonizers. Vitoria applied the *jus gentium* in condemning the actions
of the *Conquistadores* in America, arguing that the *jus gentium* forbids
taking the property of the Indians, or trying to bring them under
domination by the Spanish Empire, since they have a right to their
own government. Native Americans may not be enslaved since they
have dominion over themselves and over things, and their state of
freedom is indicated by their political systems, magistrates, system of
exchange and religion; and it is unjust to force the Christian religion
on them, since faith has to be voluntary.[35]

The apparent ambiguity in the duplicate appearance of "fornication" and "usury" in two Suarezian categories can be explained in
terms of the quality of conscientiousness or depth of ethical sensitiv-
ity. The understanding of the issues of fornication and usury in the
first of the two categories can be informed and deepened by reflection

---

[32] See above, note 1.

[33] See *The Natural Law* (St. Louis: Herder, 1947), 67. "*Lex naturalis*" here seems to
connote something like "ethnic codes of behavior."

[34] Suarez, I, ii, §§4–5.

[35] Francisco Vitoria, *De Indis et De iure belli: Relectiones*, Ernest Nys, ed. (New York:
Oceana, 1964).

on Scriptural references and religious traditions, and also by experiences contributing to maturity of conscience. A lack of religious background or a lack of life experiences could engender the limitations associated with the latter lack of depth in understanding.

Like Aquinas, Suarez recognizes a grounding of the natural law in the three fundamental inclinations of human nature, but with some modifications. Suarez downplays what Aquinas referred to as the "commonality" of humans with animals and all beings, and describes the grounding in terms of three different aspects of human nature—individuality, mortality, and rationality:

> Man is (as it were) an individual entity and as such has an inclination to preserve his own being, and to safeguard his own welfare; he is also a being corruptible—that is to say, mortal—and as such is inclined towards the preservation of the species, and towards the actions necessary to that end; and finally, he is a rational being and as such is suited for immortality, for spiritual perfection, and for communication with God and social intercourse with rational creatures. Hence, the natural law brings man to perfection, with regard to every one of his tendencies and, in this capacity, it contains various precepts—for example, precepts of temperance and of fortitude, relating to the first tendency mentioned above; those of chastity and prudence, relating to the second tendency; and those of religion, justice and so forth, relating to the third tendency.[36]

Suarez's reference to the inclination "towards the actions necessary" to the end of preserving the human species is rather conspicuously indefinite. No doubt he is referring to sexual intercourse and the education of progeny. But other means of preserving the species could also be implied—for example: fighting disease or caring for the environment. His reference to the inclinations associated with being an individual, a member of the species, and rational, are connected with specific moral virtues emphasized in the Aristotelian and Scholastic school of thought—temperance and fortitude being concerned with preserving individual life and survival in general; chastity with preserving the species; prudence with the use of reason for social harmony and spiritual development.

Suarez, like Aquinas, considers the various civil laws made by competent authorities to be valid in their own right, but not directly

---

[36] Suarez, II, viii, §4, 219.

inferred from natural law. But in cases where these positive laws conflict with or contradict natural law, positive law is superseded, and can even be nullified.

> No inferior can impose an obligation that is contrary to the law and the will of his superior; but a law prescribing a wrongful act, is contrary to the law of God, Who prohibits that act; therefore, [the former law] cannot be binding, for it is not possible that men should be bound, at one and the same time, to do and to abstain from doing a given thing.[37]

Something like "passive resistance" would be allowed in cases where civil laws clearly conflict with God's law. But like Aquinas, Suarez does not go so far as to say that serious discrepancies with the natural law can justify revolution. This was the final step taken by John Locke and others.

---

[37] Suarez, I, ix, §4, 107.

3

Grotius to Kant

The traditional scholastic hierarchy of eternal → divine → natural → human law portrayed natural law as a participation or reflection of the eternal law, inciting humans at best to a voluntary implementation of the ontological, biological, and rational *telos* of human nature. The English theologian, **Richard Hooker** (1553–1600), the "Anglican Aquinas," a major influence in the political philosophy of John Locke, largely expounded the same scholastic hierarchy. But the natural-law theory of the Dutch jurist, Hugo **Grotius** (1583–1645) began to construe both "nature" and the "divine law" somewhat differently from the scholastic tradition.

Hugo Grotius

The law of nature is a dictate of right reason, which points out that an act, according as it is or is not in conformity with rational nature, has in it a quality of moral baseness or moral necessity; . . . In this characteristic the law of nature differs not only from human law, but also from volitional divine law; for volitional divine law does not enjoin or forbid those things which in themselves and by their own nature are obligatory or not permissible, but by forbidding things it makes them unlawful, and by commanding things it makes them obligatory.[1]

---

[1] Hugo Grotius, *De Jure Belli ac Pacis Libri Tres,* trans. Francis Kelsey (New York: Oceana, 1964), I, Chapter 1, x, §§1–2.

In Grotius's analysis, we notice 1) that the emphasis is not specifically on conformity with nature, but to conformity with *rational nature*, not with animal nature or to nature ontologically considered; 2) "Volitional divine law" is not the eternal law that Aquinas and others suppose as the fountainhead of natural law, and not instances of the natural law incorporated in the divine law, but commands or prohibitions divinely imposed (possibly interpreted by ecclesiastical authorities) which go *beyond* natural law. Grotius's distinction of "volitional divine law" from the "law of nature" is somewhat similar to the distinction by Hebrew exegetes of *hukim* (laws in the Old Testament that were binding simply because they were imposed by God) from *mishpatim* (laws that admitted of rational explanation).

> We should not hastily class with the things forbidden by nature those with regard to which this point is not sufficiently clear, and which are rather prohibited by the law of the Divine Will. In this class we may perhaps place unions not classed as marriages and those which are called incestuous as well as usury.[2]

Thus non-marital cohabitation and usury may not be obvious infractions of the natural law, but are nevertheless wrong because of divine "positive" law. Grotius doesn't clarify what he means by "incestuous unions," but we may conjecture that this would include unions between cousins, probably not parent-child unions, which would require no special interdiction by volitional divine law. (Some texts read "some which . . ." instead of "those which . . .")

In addition to the distinction between issues of natural law and divine law, Grotius also refers to distinctions between general principles of the natural law and various degrees of inferences or applications:

> We should carefully distinguish between general principles, as, for example, that one must live honourably, that is, according to reason, and certain principles akin to these, but so evident that they do not admit of doubt, as that one must not seize what belongs to another, and inferences; such inferences in some cases easily gain recognition, as that, for example, accepting marriage we cannot admit adultery, but in other cases are not so easily accepted, as the inference that vengeance which is satisfied with the pain of another is wicked.[3]

---

[2] Grotius, II, Chapter 20, §§41f.
[3] *Ibid.*

The idea that natural law might be valid and binding even if God did not exist had been suggested before Grotius—for example, by Robert Bellarmine and other scholastics.[4] But Grotius made this point more explicitly and forcibly, and is frequently credited with the groundbreaking proto-modern attempt to disengage natural law from the question of the existence of a Divine Legislator:

> What we have been saying would have a degree of validity even if we should concede that which cannot be conceded without the utmost wickedness, that there is no God, or that the affairs of men are of no concern to Him.[5]

After having indicated, in this often-cited passage, the independence of his natural-law theory from any essential religious or theological moorings, Grotius goes on to explain that, even if, *per impossibile*, there were no God, elements of a natural law would still be in place, largely because of the social nature of humans and the necessity of maintaining civilized relationships.

> Man is, to be sure, an animal, but an animal of a superior kind, much farther removed from all other animals than the different kinds of animals are from one another. . . . Among the traits characteristic of man is an impelling desire for society, that is, for social life—not of any and every sort, but peaceful, and organized according to the measure of his intelligence, with those who are of his own kind; . . . therefore the assertion that every animal is impelled by nature to seek only its own good cannot be conceded. . . . Maintenance of the social order, which we have roughly sketched, and which is consonant with human intelligence, is the source of law properly so called. . . . Over other animals man has the advantage of possessing not only a strong bent towards social life, of which we have spoken, but also a power of discrimination which enables him to decide what things are agreeable or harmful (as to both things present and things to come).[6]

Thus Grotius sets himself in opposition to the position of the Greek skeptic, Carneades, who asserted that "every animal is impelled by nature to seek only its own good." Grotius takes the intrinsically

---

[4] See Crowe, *The Changing Profile of Natural Law*, 223–28.
[5] Grotius, Prolegomena §11.
[6] Grotius, Prolegomena §§6–9.

social, altruistic nature of rational beings as the pivotal principle on which the dictates of natural law hinge—even if there were no God. Consistently with this emphasis on sociality, the distinctions of natural-law directives that Grotius elaborates have largely to do with greater or less relevance to maintenance of the social order.[7]

Grotius, the "father of international law," also considers the relevance of natural law to the domains of civil and international law, resulting in an expanded hierarchy (see the facing page).

Thomas Hobbes

The English philosopher **Thomas Hobbes** (1588–1679) is not generally considered a proponent of natural-law theory, but as a "state of nature" theorist, infamous for his pessimistic description of the original human condition as a "war of every man, against every man," in which life is "solitary, poor, nasty, brutish, and short." But he does analyze natural law in detail, as an offshoot of his "state of nature" theory. Hobbes's fundamental natural-law principle is the principle of self-preservation on the part of individuals who are not necessarily antisocial or unsocial, but more precisely pre-social. Thus Hobbes is seriously at odds with Grotius and others who emphasize the natural sociability and fellow-feeling of humans.[8] Hobbes describes at length the natural-law implications of this basic position in *De Cive*:

> We do not . . . by nature seek society for its own sake, but that we may receive some honour or profit from it; these we desire primarily, that secondarily. . . . The *law of nature*, that I may define it, is the dictate of right reason, conversant about those things which are either to be done or omitted for the constant preservation of life and members, as much as in us lies. . . . The first and fundamental law of nature is, *that peace is to be sought after, where it may be found; and where not, there to provide ourselves for helps of war.*[9]

---

[7] Grotius, Prolegomena §6.
[8] Hobbes is usually classified meta-ethically as an "ethical egoist," although some dispute this view. See Robert Shaver, *Hobbes* (Aldershot: Ashgate, 1999), 273–308.
[9] Thomas Hobbes, *De Cive*, trans. Hobbes, ed. Bernard Gert (Indianapolis: Hackett, 1991), I, 2, 111.

Volitional divine law	Examples: The prohibition of usury, non-marital cohabitation, and some forms of incest.
General principles	Examples: Everyone must live honorably, that is, according to reason; we must not take what belongs to another.
Inferences that easily gain recognition	Example: Marriage vows are incompatible with adultery; restoring to another any property of his that we may have, together with any gain which we may have received from it; fulfilling promises; making good of losses incurred through our fault; penalizing evil-doing.
Inferences that are more difficult to make.	Example: Awareness that vengeance which is satisfied with the pain of another person is wicked.
Natural law supplemented by the will of men	Example: Institutions of private property and distributive justice, superseding primitive communistic societies
The "law of nations," which can sometimes legitimately diverge from natural law for the advancement of civilization	Examples: Institution of slavery; tacit acceptance of tyranny as a pragmatic social contract.
Positive law, which can permit actions forbidden by the natural law, or forbid actions allowed by the natural law	Examples: Permitting the "law of the stronger" in war in contravention of the natural law of peaceful coexistence; forbidding polygamy, which the natural law allows.

From these premises, Hobbes goes on to derive a second law of nature, to "*perform contracts,* or *to keep trust,*" and a third precept that one should "accept not a gift, but with a mind to endeavour that the giver shall have no just occasion to repent him of his gift." Further derivations include precepts that men should be useful to one another, not hold grudges, avoid cruel retaliation, avoid showing scorn or hatred to others, and treat others as equal—even though they may *not* be equal![10]

Hobbes emphasizes that these are "laws" only analogically. They are simply natural responses to the original need for self-preservation, resulting in a "social contract" and the political and interpersonal ramifications necessary to stabilize and perpetuate that contract. In order for them to be considered laws in the strict sense, we would have to hold that they are commanded by God in Holy Scripture.[11]

In Hobbes's estimation, natural laws, geared to assuring a relatively stable and secure exit from the fearful state of nature, help to preserve life; but they offer no assurance of a peaceful existence, because of the unpredictability of human responses:

> If perhaps some, more humble than the rest, should exercise that equity and usefulness which reason dictates, the others not practising the same, surely they would not follow reason in so doing: nor would they hereby procure themselves peace, but a more certain quick destruction. . . .[12]

Thus for Hobbes natural law is by no means strict and exceptionless. We are dispensed from following the natural law whenever involved in social circumstances wherein others would take advantage of our compliance. Hobbesian natural law leaves us with the image of a social reciprocity governed by the principle, "scratch my back, and I'll scratch yours," but overshadowed by anxiety about actually turning your back to a fellow citizen.

---

[10] *Ibid.*
[11] Hobbes, III, 33, 152.
[12] Hobbes, III, 27, 148.

Richard Cumberland

Richard Cumberland (1631–1718), an Anglican bishop, viewed Hobbes's theory as morally dangerous because of its dim view of human propensities, and epistemologically weak because Hobbesian "rights" can only be understood in the context of the priority of the common good.[13] Cumberland and other natural-law theorists of the eighteenth century were motivated to develop an ethical alternative, an antidote to both the mistaken presuppositions and the flawed methodology of Hobbes.

Cumberland, influenced by the great admiration for mathematics characteristic of that era, advocated a "science of ethics" based on analytic procedures. He portrays ethical life-choices as analogous to acceptable and effective mathematical procedures. Just as in working out an algebra problem we have a general idea of the result which gets clearer and clearer as we follow standard operations in solving it, so also in using our human faculties we start with an indefinite idea of happiness which becomes more specific and concrete as we continue acting, like an effect resulting necessarily from its causes.[14] Using such procedures, we arrive at a natural law that leads out of Hobbesian egoism[15] into altruism, and a basic principle that shows a *prima facie* similarity to what later became called utilitarianism:

> The greatest benevolence of every rational agent towards all, forms the happiest state of every, and of all the benevolent, as far as is in their power, and is necessarily requisite to the happiest state which they can attain, and therefore the common good is the supreme law.[16]

---

[13] Richard Cumberland, *A Philosophical Inquiry into the Laws of Nature, &c. and A Confutation of the Elements of Mr. Hobbes's Philosophy*, in *A Treatise of the Laws of Nature*, trans. John Maxwell, (New York: Garland, 1978), I, §23, 67.

[14] Cumberland, IV, 4, §3, 186. The algebraic analogy in morals is also found in Grotius, Pufendorf, and Locke. See Pauline Westerman, "Hume and the Natural Lawyers: a Change of Landscape," in Stewart and Wright eds., *Hume and Hume's Connexions* (University Park: Pennsylvania State University Press, 1994), 86.

[15] As mentioned above (p. 34n), the common interpretation of Hobbes as an ethical egoist has been challenged. See A.E. Taylor, "The Ethical Doctrine of Hobbes," *Philosophy* 13 (1938), 406–424, and Howard Warrender, *The Political Philosophy of Hobbes: His Theory of Obligation* (Oxford: Clarendon, 1957), who maintains that Hobbes's ascription of natural-law obligations to individuals is conceptually prior to obligatoriness emerging from the sovereign.

[16] Cumberland, V, 1, 189.

But we can see from this statement that Cumberland goes considerably beyond the classical utilitarian maxim of producing "the greatest happiness for the greatest number." As he elaborates on his conception of happiness, it takes on global proportions both qualitatively and quantitatively:

> Whereas the end proposed by every one is that entire and greatest good, which he can procure to the universe and to himself in his station, it follows that the end is to be conceived as the greatest aggregate or sum of good effects, most acceptable to God and men, which can be effected by the greatest industry of all our future actions, . . . whence arises a vast increase, both of public and private happiness beyond what can be distinctly foreseen.[17]

Cumberland argues that this is not a hopelessly idealistic vision, but a goal fully in accord with the way that humans are "determined by some sort of natural necessity to pursue good foreseen, especially the greatest [good], and to avoid evils.[18] And just as in civil laws there are sanctions to make the laws efficacious, so also there are natural sanctions which tend to promote progress in attainment of universal good:

> The endeavour, to the utmost of our power, of promoting the common good of the whole system of rational agents conduces, as far as in us lies, to the good of every part, in which our own happiness as that of a part is contained. But contrary actions produce contrary effects, and consequently our own misery, among that of others.[19]

Cumberland, like Cicero, argues for the existence of internal, presumably private, penalties resulting from infractions of the natural law. The question as to whether there are such sanctions will be further examined in Chapter 6.

Samuel Pufendorf

The German philosopher **Samuel Pufendorf** (1632–1694), like Cumberland, presupposes the sociability of humans, but with residual

---

[17] Cumberland, IV, 4, §3, 186.
[18] Cumberland, V, 27, 233.
[19] Cumberland, Introduction, IX.

Hobbesian nuances, as if to correct an exaggerated altruism in Cumberland. He emphasizes the capacity of men to be sociable, not their intrinsically social nature:

> The fundamental natural law is: every man ought to do as much as he can to cultivate and preserve sociability. . . . Man . . . is an animal with an intense concern for his own preservation, needy by himself, incapable of protection without the help of his fellows, and very well fitted for the mutual provision of benefits. Equally, however, he is at the same time malicious, aggressive, easily provoked and as willing as he is able to inflict harm on others. The conclusion is: in order to be safe, it is necessary for him to be sociable; that is to join forces with men like himself and so conduct himself towards them that they are not given even a plausible excuse for harming him, but rather become willing to preserve and promote his advantages.[20]

From these general principles, which have to do with the human need for society, Pufendorf deduces a set of absolute and conditional duties that are all concerned with the attainment of universal happiness. The absolute duties in descending order are 1) "not to harm others";[21] 2) "[let] each man value and treat the other as naturally his equal, or as equally a man";[22] 3) "everyone should be useful to others, so far as he conveniently can"[23] The "conditional" duties have to do with mutual agreements which result in rules, contracts and conventions to assure and maintain sociability and mutual trust.[24]

Using the primacy of interpersonal relations as his springboard, and requiring a belief in God as the lawgiver to justify obligations connected with human nature, Pufendorf goes on to deduce duties to oneself, as well as to others:

> In natural liberty, if you do away with fear of the Deity, as soon as anyone has confidence in his own strength, he will inflict whatever he wishes on those weaker than himself, and treat goodness, shame and good faith as

---

[20] Samuel Pufendorf, *On the Duty of Man and Citizen, according to Natural Law* (New York: Cambridge, 1991), I, 3, §7, 35.
[21] Pufendorf, I, 6, §2, 56.
[22] Pufendorf, I, 7, §1. 61
[23] Pufendorf, I, 8, §1, 64
[24] Pufendorf, I, 9, §2, 68

empty words; and will have no other motive to do right than the sense of his own weakness. The internal cohesion of states also would be perpetually insecure if religion were abolished [25]. . . . No one gave himself life; it must be regarded as a gift of God. Hence it is clear that man certainly does not have power over his own life to the extent that he may terminate it at his pleasure. . . . Yet it may be quite correct for a man to choose what will probably shorten his life in order to make his talents more widely available to others. . . . Again, since a citizen must often risk his own life to save the lives of many others he may be ordered by his legitimate ruler under threat of the severest penalties not to avoid danger by flight. He may also take such a risk of his own accord provided that there are not stronger arguments against it and there is reason to expect that his action will result in safety for others and that they deserve to be saved at so high a price.[26]

Noteworthy in this deduction is the somewhat pragmatic-sounding argument concerning religion—almost reminiscent of J.S. Mill's *The Utility of Religion*, although it is clear that Pufendorf himself had strong religious commitments. His insistence on duties to oneself—a problematic issue in a natural-law theory based on human sociality—is bolstered by the non-pragmatic religious belief that life is a gift to each individual from God.

Immanuel Kant

Although **Immanuel Kant** (1724–1804) is not a natural-law theorist, he discusses the meaning and classification of natural law from what might be called a "phenomenological" point of view—that is, with an emphasis on determining the proper subjective stance with regard to something that has a *prima facie* claim to objectivity and reality:

> Obligatory laws for which an external legislation is possible are called generally external laws. Those external laws, the obligatoriness of which can be recognized by reason *a priori* even without an external legislation, are called natural laws. Those laws, again, which are not obligatory with-

---

[25] Pufendorf, I, 4, §9, 43.
[26] Pufendorf, I, 5, §4, 47.

out actual external legislation, are called positive laws. An external legislation, containing pure natural laws, is therefore conceivable; but in that case a previous natural law must be presupposed to establish the authority of the lawgiver by the right to subject others to obligation through his own act of will. The principle which makes a certain action a duty is a practical law.[27]

The Kant scholar, Hans **Vaihinger** (1852–1933), summed up the philosophy of Kant as a "philosophy as-if"—dealing with helpful, leading ideas like God and things-in-themselves as if they were objective realities. The text just cited indicates that the "as if" interpretation is applicable also to Kant's moral philosophy: Natural laws prevailing in an external code are "conceivable"; but only if we presuppose a previous natural law establishing the authority of their lawgiver; and we could not presuppose this unless there was a prior "practical law" laying down the principle for the obligatoriness of this law. Thus we end up with three orders of natural law:

First-order natural law—NL_1	"x ought to do y"
Second-order natural law—NL_2	"NL_1 ought to be authorized by NL_2
Third-order natural law—NL_3	"NL_2 ought to be made authoritative by a general practical law"

Kant himself brings out the "as if" nature of natural law explicitly and verbatim in his first formulation of the Categorical Imperative, *Act only on that maxim whereby thou canst at the same time will that it should become a universal law,* when he immediately adds, with reference to natural law, the following proviso:

Since the universality of the law according to which effects are produced constitutes what is properly called *nature* in the most general sense (as to form)—that is, the existence of things so far as it is determined by gen-

---

[27] Immanuel Kant, *Introduction to a Metaphysic of Morals*, Part IV.

eral laws—the imperative of duty may be expressed thus: *Act as if the maxim of thy action were to become by thy will a universal law of nature.*[28]

If any doubt could remain as to Kant's position regarding the reality of natural law, he dispels these doubts in his discussion of whether a basis for moral law can be found empirically in human nature itself:

> Everyone must admit that if a law is to have moral force, that is, to be the basis of an obligation, it must carry with it absolute necessity. . . . The basis of obligation must not be sought in the nature of man, or in the circumstances in the world in which he is placed, but *a priori* simply in the conceptions of pure reason; and although any other precept which is founded on principles of mere experience may be in certain respects universal, yet in as far as it rests even in the least degree on an empirical basis, perhaps only as to a motive, such a precept, while it may be a practical rule, can never be called a moral law.[29]

In contemporary moral theory, as we shall see in the next chapter, we find in some schools of thought similar attempts to ground natural law purely in human reason, rather than in "nature." Possibly the best way to understand the moral principles that issue from these theories is that, like the Kantian Categorical Imperative, they are proposed not as principles of natural law, but *as if* they were principles of natural law. Like Kant, they consider "nature" to be completely extrinsic to reason, and thus of no moral value. Thus the task facing them is, using reason alone, to develop a satisfactory replacement for the allegedly objective validity of natural law.

---

[28] *Fundamental Principles of a Metaphysic of Morals,* trans. Thomas K. Abbot (Indianapolis: Bobbs-Merrill, 1963), 38.
[29] *Ibid.*, 5.

4

Contemporary Developments
in Natural Law

A common criticism of natural-law theories is that they are ambiguous, unwieldy, and prone to inflated claims. As Jeremy Bentham (1748–1832) put it,

> A great multitude of people are continually talking of the Law of Nature; and then they go on giving you their [personal] sentiments about what is right and what is wrong; and these sentiments, you are to understand, are so many chapters, and sections of the Law of Nature. . . . [The "Natural Law" consists] in so many contrivances for avoiding the obligation of appealing to any external standard, and for prevailing upon the readers to accept of the author's sentiment or opinion as a reason, and that a sufficient one, for itself.[1]

H.L.A. Hart echoes these judgments, charging that

> Natural law theory in all its protean guises attempts to assert that human beings are equally devoted to and united in their conception of aims (the pursuit of knowledge, justice to their fellow men) other than that of survival.[2]

---

[1] Jeremy Bentham, *An Introduction to the Principles of Morals and Legislation*, ed. J.H. Burns, and H.L.A. Hart (New York: Methuen, 1982), Chapter 1.
[2] H.L.A. Hart, "Positivism and the Separation of Law and Morals," *Harvard Law Review* 71 (1958), 593.

While Bentham expressed concern that any nostrum could be rationalized under the pseudo-external standard, "natural law," Hart criticizes natural law for boasting a false consensus, ignoring the fact that there is such a vast relativity in moral values in humankind that no "common denominator" could be found. It is interesting that Hart makes an exception for "survival" as a pursuit or value for which there does seem to be an almost universal consensus.

If natural law makes any claim, it is a claim to objectivity, not being influenced by whims, caprices, or self-interest. But this is precisely what Ernest Van den Haag calls into doubt:

> Just as some philosophers inferred from natural law that slavery is wrong, others, particularly in antiquity (Aristotle among them), found that slavery is justified by natural law. Just as some will deduce from natural law that women are equal to men and ought to be treated as equals, others concluded that women are inferior and should be subordinated to men. Similarly, capital punishment can be opposed or supported on natural-law grounds.[3]

Modern American Currents in Natural-Law Thought

In spite of such criticisms, and the deontological and consequentialist alternatives introduced by Kant, Bentham, and others, elements of natural-law thinking have perdured for the last two centuries. The American Constitution, with its emphasis on human equality and self-evident rights to life, liberty and the pursuit of happiness, was influenced by Locke's state-of-nature theory. According to Christopher Wolfe, currents of natural law have remained in American judicial thinking up to the present in Lockean-inspired laissez-faire court developments, emphasizing property rights; in Justice Felix Frankfurter's emphasis on the history and traditions of Anglo-American law; and in metaethical theories *about* law which supersede, and offer criteria for, positive law."[4]

---

[3] Ernest Van den Haag, "Not above the Law," *National Review* 43 (1991), 25, 27.
[4] Christopher Wolfe, "Judicial Review," in David Forte, ed., *Natural Law and Contemporary Public Policy* (Washington, D.C.: Georgetown University Press, 1998), 157ff.

In the twentieth century, the Thomistic approach to natural law has been carried forth by Jacques Maritain, Yves Simon, Thomas Davitt, and, more recently Henry Veatch, Ralph McInerny, and Russell Hittinger, among others. Outside this tradition, H.L.A. Hart, although a legal positivist, allows for the possibility of a natural law of "survival"; and with survival in mind, Hart offers what he designates as the "minimum content of natural law"—provision for "natural necessities" in view of human vulnerability; maintaining approximate human equality; safeguards for property; and the imposition of sanctions when necessary.[5] Such "necessities" might better fit into the category of fundamental policy considerations in a democracy. Hart also offers "secondary rules" related to this "minimal content"—rules concerning modification of laws, adjudication, etc.—which are obviously concerned with legal procedures, and not related to natural law in the traditional sense.

Lon Fuller's counter-proposal to Hart's "survival" is a natural law of "maintenance of communication" with regard to legislation and the promulgation of law;[6] implementation of this communication-principle would combat eight procedural sources of disaster in lawmaking: 1) failure to achieve rules, emphasis on *ad hoc* decisions; 2) failure to publicize; 3) abuse of retroactive legislation; 4) failure to make rules understandable; 5) the enactment of contradictory rules, or 6) rules that require conduct beyond the powers of the affected party; 7) introducing too frequent changes in laws; and 8) lack of congruence between announced rules and the way they are administered. But Fuller's proposal, like Hart's "secondary rules," seems similarly to regard matters of jurisprudence in a narrower, technical sense, not natural law. Kenneth Einar observes that Fuller's criteria refer to a legal system, rather than particular laws within a system, and are concerned with proper functioning of that system, an internal teleology that is essentially connected with efficient legislation, but which is not necessarily moral.[7]

---

[5] H.L.A. Hart, "Philosophy of Law and Jurisprudence in Britain (1945–1952)," *American Journal of Comparative Law* (1953); and *The Concept of Law*, 189.
[6] See Fuller, 25.
[7] Kenneth Einar, "Functionalism and Legal Theory: the Hart-Fuller Debate Revisited," in *De philosophia* 14 (1998), 213–232.

In addition to the political and religious events mentioned in the Introduction to this book, developments in ethical theory have also instigated renewed critical interest in natural law theory. As Lisska notes,[8] the catalysts in recent decades for this renewed interest include Elizabeth Anscombe's 1958 article on "Modern Moral Philosophy," raising the issue of the possible relevance of psychology to moral theory, and Alasdair MacIntyre's 1981 book, *After Virtue*, arguing that modern moral philosophy has gotten completely away from the fundamental issues discussed by Aristotle.

The "New Natural Law" Theory

A major hurdle, however, hindering the further development of natural-law thinking, consists of some more or less standard requirements in contemporary ethics—namely, maintaining the distinction between values and facts, avoiding the "naturalistic fallacy" interdicted by G.E. Moore, and observing the Humean prohibition against deriving an "ought" from an "is."[9] In the resultant, conscientious effort of developing a natural-law philosophy which starts with intelligible values rather than facts, and studiously avoids deriving any ethical conclusions from empirical facts about "human nature," analytic philosophers Germain Grisez and John Finnis have taken the lead; in particular, Finnis's book, *Natural Law and Natural Rights*,[10] written with the support of Finnis's mentor, H.L.A. Hart (with whose views of law Finnis differs markedly), has taken the limelight as a new approach to natural law which conforms to prevailing standards for ethical theory.

Both Grisez and Finnis start from a set of self-evident basic values, from which by logical inference rational people can arrive at the "natural laws" of individual and social conduct. Grisez lists eight "modes of responsibility," including: working for intelligible goods, avoiding moral decision-making on the basis of mere emotion, avoiding conflict among intelligible goods, etc.; Grisez connects these eight modes

---

[8] Lisska, *Aquinas's Theory of Natural Law* (Oxford: Clarendon, 1996), 1.

[9] For a discussion of these issues, see Chapter 6 below.

[10] *Natural Law and Natural Rights* (Oxford:Clarendon, 1980); hereafter abbreviated as *NLNR*.

with the Eight Beatitudes of the Gospels and the tradition of the "gifts of the Holy Spirit" in Christian tradition.[11] Finnis's list, coinciding with some of Grisez's "modes of responsibility," has evolved over the years. Finnis's early list included

> Living, in health and some security; the acquisition of arts and skills to be cultivated for their own sake; the relishing of beauty; the seeking of knowledge and understanding; the cultivation of friendships, immediate, communal and political; effective and intelligent freedom; a right relation in this passing life to the lasting principles of reality, "the gods"; the procreation of children and their education so that they can attain for themselves, and in their own mode, the foregoing values.[12]

Finnis's final revised list of basic values enumerated seven objectives or forms of the good, to which other pursuits seem to be subordinate: 1) Knowledge; 2) life; 3) play; 4) aesthetic experience; 5) sociability (friendship); 6) practical reasonableness (applying one's intelligence to problems and situations); 7) religion and pursuit of ultimate questions about the cosmos and life.[13]

Examining this list closely, we see that the "goods" listed are not moral goods in the strict sense, but at best pre-moral—for example play and aesthetic experience are not usually put into the category of morality, and the connection of sociability with morality seems less than obvious. We should also notice that while practical reasonableness is listed as just one of the seven goods, it is potentially applicable to or associated with all of the other goods, like the Aristotelian virtue of "prudence." In actual practice, Finnis in his analyses seems to treat practical reasonableness as "more equal than" the other equal goods.

How can we justify this selection of pivotal primary values? Finnis considers each of them a self-evident good. Observing that there are self-evident truths in geometry, and that the natural sciences self-evidently are based on the principles of elementary formal logic, he goes on to argue:

---

[11] Germain Grisez, *Christian Moral Principles*, Vol. I of Grisez's *The Way of the Lord Jesus* (Chicago: Franciscan Herald Press, 1983), 225-26.

[12] John Finnis, "Natural Law and Unnatural Acts," *Heythrop Journal* 11 (1970), 365–387.

[13] *NLNR*, 86–90

It may be still more helpful, for the purposes of this brief reflection on self-evidence, to consider some of the principles or norms of sound judgment in every empirical discipline. . . . One such principle is that the principles of logic, for example the forms of deductive inference, are to be used and adhered to in all one's thinking, even though no non-circular proof of their validity is possible (since any proof would employ them). Another is that an adequate reason why anything is so rather than otherwise is to be expected, unless one has a reason not to expect such a reason. . . . A third is that self-defeating theses are to be abandoned. . . . A fourth is that phenomena are to be regarded as real unless there is some reason to distinguish between appearance and reality. . . . Such principles of theoretical rationality are not demonstrable, for they are presupposed or deployed in anything that we would count as a demonstration. . . . They are objective.[14]

In other words, by means of pure logical analysis, avoidance of self-contradiction and the proper distinction of appearance from reality, we can discern that the basic values are indeed self-evident. Finnis uses the value of knowledge as his illustrative example of how a basic value can be self-evident. The assertion that knowledge is an intrinsic good cannot be proven, Finnis maintains, for example from the fact that, as Aristotle noted, "all men desire to know." Even if this is a true fact, it does not generate self-evidence. Rather, it is self-evident because all acts of knowledge or attempts at knowledge include procedures for avoiding or limiting the possibilities of ignorance. Even skeptics, denying this proposition, are in practice asserting the value of the skeptical conclusion which they *know*.[15]

Finnis goes to great length here, in a chapter comprising several thousand words, arguing that the self-evidence of the value of knowledge is not based on consensus or on feelings of certitude or on natural desires, but on purely logical considerations; but the reader is left with the question why, if this proposition is so self-evident, such lengthy expatiations are necessary. Some of Finnis's critics have focused primarily on this claim of self-evidence.

Prima facie some of Finnis's seven basic values might seem to be related to elements of the Thomistic triad—the value of "life" is relevant to self-preservation or to procreation, the value of "knowledge"

---

[14] *NLNR*, 68–69
[15] *NLNR*, 70-75

to the development of one's rational powers. But for both Grisez and Finnis, the Thomistic triad is a *bête noire*, from which they wish to distance themselves completely.

> [Grisez] became convinced that Thomas's account of the ultimate end is inconsistent with his account of natural law. This conviction led him to develop his own ethical theory, which is heavily indebted to Thomas but which is autonomously grounded.[16]

The problem is that Aquinas, in discussing the basic human inclinations, does seem to derive fundamental principles of natural law from this basis in human nature. So if Grisez touches on some of the same values considered by Aquinas, it must be understood that they are *not* derived from reflections on human nature. Finnis also makes it clear that he does not have any derivation in mind.

> [Regarding Aquinas's discussion of the triad of inclinations[17] in human nature:] All this is no doubt true, and quite pertinent in a metaphysical meditation on the continuity of human order with the universal order-of-things (of which human nature is a microcosmos, incorporating all levels of being: inorganic, organic, . . . mental . . .) But is it relevant to a meditation on the *value* of the various basic aspects of human well-being?[18]

Debatable Issues

This disengagement from "metaphysics" has become a matter of contention among Thomists outside the analytic tradition. Shortly after the appearance of *Natural Law and Natural Right*, Vernon Bourke criticized the complete disregard of the metaphysics of finality—"[Finnis and Grisez] speak of the ends of human choices but they pay no attention to the end of human life."[19] Veatch, in his journal review following

---

[16] "The Basic Principles of Natural Law: A Reply to Ralph McInerny," in C. Curran and R.A. McCormick, S.J., eds., *Readings in Moral Theology No. 7: Natural Law and Theology* (New York: Paulist Press, 1991), 167.

[17] See above, page 29.

[18] *NLNR*, 94.

[19] Vernon Bourke, "Finnis's Natural Law and Natural Rights," *American Journal of Jurisprudence* 26 (1981), 245.

the initial appearance of Finnis's book, voices the now-common criticism of Finnis's theory, that it is a "natural law without nature":

> It really isn't necessary, [Finnis] seems to say, that so-called natural laws in law and in ethics be laws of nature at all, or in any sense discoverable in nature. Yes, and as if to puzzle and perplex his readers even more, Finnis apparently wants to claim no less a one than St. Thomas Aquinas as being on his side in this regard. For St. Thomas, Finnis suggests, was one who was never taken in by any such notion as that one might be able to derive ethical principles from nature, or that one would ever need to suppose that ethics had to be based on metaphysics. . . . Could it be that he [Finnis] was somehow tempted by the devil, so as to seem to say that natural law doctrines are not really based on a knowledge of nature after all![20]

Ralph McInerny argues that the self-evident principles on which Grisez and Finnis base their moral theory are completely outside the category of morality.

> The first underived self-evident principles [for Finnis and Grisez], the precepts of natural law, are pre-moral, not moral. Moral principles are nonetheless derived from them. What this comes down to, in terms of [the *Summa*, q. 94, a.2] is the claim that the basic values, the goods pointed to or aimed at by the instincts, are not as such moral values. . . . The basic values that Finnis lists, expanding a bit on Grisez . . . are not moral values, singly, or cumulatively. [As Finnis says, *Natural Law and Natural Right*, p. 59:] "Neither this chapter nor the next makes or presupposes any moral judgments. Rather, these two chapters concern the evaluative substratum of all judgments. That is to say, they concern the acts of practical understanding in which we grasp the basic values of human existence and thus, too, the basic principles of all practical reasoning." Grisez [speaks of] these self-evident principles of natural law as pre-moral. He seems more concerned to have principles that will govern the practical activity of all men, good or bad, and which thus must split the difference between moral and immoral. If the bad man as well as the good is guided by these first principles the one will not be called good nor the other bad simply because he is guided by them.[21]

---

[20] Henry Veatch, "Finnis's *Natural Law and Natural Rights*," *The American Journal of Jurisprudence* 26 (1981), 256.
[21] Curran and McCormick, *Readings in Moral Theology*, 148.

Thus while Finnis dismisses Aquinas's reference to fundamental human inclinations as interesting metaphysical speculations which have no special relevance to morality, McInerny finds Finnis's self-evident basic values to be an unsatisfactory replacement—if a replacement were needed. Finnis's basic premises have been also subjected to criticism by others outside the Thomistic tradition.

Robert Scavone finds Finnis's theory weakest in the area where its chief strength is claimed—in its faithfulness to logical analysis.

> The logical underpinnings of [Finnis's] theory are seriously flawed, and the connections linking the self-evidence of value to the necessity, function, and moral force of law are weak and often untenable. Despite the power of his local insight, the flaws vitiate Finnis's claims that the values are pre-moral and equally basic, that the good of "practical reasonableness" logically gives rise to a moral duty to follow its requirements. . . .[22]

Scavone observes that Finnis describes the moral obligations associated with his theory as at most what Kant would call hypothetical imperatives:

> The problem . . . lies with the hypothetical nature of the imperatives that result from the supposition that this value is only one among equals: "Each of these requirements concerns what one MUST do, or think, or be, if one is to participate in the basic value of practical reasonableness" (Finnis, p. 102). . . . The "if" seems to imply that no one "must"—logically or practically—participate in this value at all.[23]

Scavone goes on to argue that an egoist, as long as he respects practical reasonableness as a basic value, could choose just to pursue the values of play and aesthetic experience. And he observes that, whereas Finnis prides himself on the objectivity of his ethical theory based on the self-evidence of the basic values, he slides patently from the objective sense of "self-evidence" to the subjective sense, with exhortatory statements such as the following from *Natural Law and Natural Right*:

---

[22] "Natural Law, Obligation, and the Common Good: What Finnis Can't Tell Us," *University of Toronto Faculty of Law Review* 43 (1985), 92
[23] *Ibid.*, 100.

Is it not the case that knowledge is really a good, an aspect of authentic human flourishing, and that the principle which expresses its value formulates a real (intelligent) reason for action? It seems clear that such indeed is the case, and that there are no sufficient reasons for doubting it to be so. The good of knowledge is self-evident, obvious. It cannot be demonstrated, but equally it needs no demonstration.[24]

Jennifer Herdt explains the subjectivism of Finnis and Grisez as an inevitable result of their insistence that there is no (natural) hierarchy among the basic goods, but the moral individual's intention never to act against a basic good prevents conflict. The simple intention of avoiding conflict is not sufficient to obviate capricious rational choices.[25]

Valerie Kerruish finds Finnis's seven basic values susceptible to extremely volatile interpretations, so as to give hardly any clear moral directives:

The good of life . . . might be interpreted either as the life of the species, including future generations, or as the life of an individual. Friendship or love might encompass individually disinterested benevolence to all of humanity or the limited egoism of relationships between individuals. Knowledge may be sought for its own sake or for enabling us (since whatever we are it is not lilies of the field) to survive and enrich our survival.[26]

Anthony Lisska in *Aquinas's Theory of Natural Law* examines the partial confluence and partial clash of Thomism and contemporary ethical theory in Finnis, and concludes that the genealogy of Finnis's theory can be traced back fairly clearly to the eighteenth-century Enlightenment and to Kant as its most important exemplar in ethics. Veatch's critique of Finnis *et al*, says Lisska, is based on the consequences of the Kantian "transcendental turn," according to which there are by definition no things-in-themselves, so that all questions turn out to be epistemological or phenomenological or existential or

---

[24] *Ibid.*, 96; citing *NLNR*, 64–65.
[25] "Free Choice, Self-Referential Arguments, and the New Natural Law," *American Catholic Philosophical Quarterly* 72 (1998), 597–600.
[26] "Philosophical Retreat: A Criticism of John Finnis's Theory of Natural Law," *University of Western Australia Law Review* 15 (1983), 227.

methodological. Both Kant and Descartes (with his *Rules for the Direction of the Mind*) emphasized method and procedure, and approach "objectivity" from the vantage point of subjective rational procedures. But, comments Veatch, this is not really objectivity.[27]

As an ethical theory, the "new natural-law theory" of Finnis and Grisez may be an important contribution in its own right, bringing to a head major ethical currents in the twentieth century, offering an alternative to utilitarianism,[28] supporting many if not most of the basic precepts connected traditionally with natural law. But the question remains—is it natural law? In order for it to be literally a *law*, one must presuppose a lawgiver, and this has traditionally been God, although natural-law theorists such as Grotius have sometimes tried to soften that connection. In order for it to be *natural*, one seems to need to presuppose some connection with, if not derivation from, nature itself, especially human nature. Both of these connections are absent in Finnis's theory.

Finnis in his chapter on law is quite clear that natural law is "law" only by way of analogy, the way that scientific theories and rules governing artistic and technical activities are sometimes called laws:

> Physical, chemical, biological, and psychological laws are only metaphorically laws. To say this is not to question the legitimacy of the discourse of natural scientists, for whose purposes, conversely, what we call "law strictly speaking" is only metaphorically a set of laws. The similarity between our central case and the laws of arts and crafts and applied sciences is greater. . . . "Natural law"—the set of principles of practical reasonableness in ordering human life and human community—is only analogically law, in relation to my present focal use of the term: that is why the term has been avoided in this chapter on Law.[29]

Finnis himself gives evidence of a certain ambivalence about a natural law without a lawgiver in his final chapter on "Nature, Reason, God," which tries very cautiously and almost apologetically to open

---

[27] Anthony Lisska, *Aquinas's Theory of Natural Law* (New York: Oxford University Press, 1996), 170–75.
[28] *NLNR*, 116.
[29] *NLNR*, 280.

up the possibility of a transcendent source of knowledge and value, since "natural reasoning . . . leaves somehow 'subjective' and 'questionable' the whole structure of basic principles and requirements of practical reasonableness and human flourishing discussed in Chapters III–XII"[!][30]

Finnis also claims that the natural-law theory of Thomas Aquinas himself is independent of any essential connection with a belief in God. This leads to the ostensibly revolutionary claim that, *pace* Grotius, Aquinas developed the first strictly *secular* natural-law theory.[31]

With regard to the connection of natural law with *nature*, Finnis would argue that his theory is indeed based on nature, that is, on practical reasonableness which is the distinctive characteristic of human nature. This argument sports a certain circularity: it is reasonable to follow reason, and this is the most natural thing for humans. Here again, Finnis finds himself at odds with the natural-law tradition, in which naturalness is distinct from, but implies reasonableness, and living in accord with nature (which is not simply identified with reason) is preeminently reasonable. Like Kant's categorical imperative, a pure product of reason which functions "as if" a law of nature, Finnis's basic rational principal values are presented "as if" they were values imbedded in nature. One could say that, like Kant, Finnis considers his rational and logical elaboration of self-evident values to confer objectivity on these values. But from the vantage point of traditional natural law, his approach seems to be one step removed from the objectivity and reality of nature.

On the other hand, what does it mean to base a moral theory on "nature"? And cannot the existence of moral laws, which are not construed as positive laws laid down by God, be justified as *bona fide* laws for human behavior and interactions, independently from association with some divine legislator? These issues will be explored in Chapter 5.

---

[30] *NLNR*, 405.
[31] Charles Covell, *The Defence of Natural Law* (New York: St. Martin's Press, 1992), 222–23.

5

Conceptual Analyses of Issues
in Natural-Law Theory

As we have seen from the preceding historical survey, "natural law" or the "law of nature" has had multiple connotations. Such divergence seems to be inevitable. Erik Wolf came to the conclusion that, in view of the varying meanings of both "nature" and "law," there are 120 conceivable definitions of natural law![1]

In view of the fact that we in the twenty-first century have exchanged formerly static views of nature for an evolutionary concept in which "human nature" is just the latest post-hominid stage in a progression of changes taking place over billions of years, can we moderns find a consensus with natural-law theorists from earlier eras? Or is it important that we do so? Perhaps the "natural" in "natural law" is synonymous with rational, and really has nothing to do with the varying concepts of nature. And what about "law"? Can natural law as a strictly philosophical theory, independent of theological commitments and the idea of a divine lawgiver, be a *law* in any meaningful way—as something promulgated for the common good, and associated with commands and penalties for infractions? With these questions in mind, we begin with a conceptual analysis of the terms "nature," "natural," and "law."

---

[1] Erik Wolf, *Das Problem der Naturrechtslehre: Versuch einer Orientierung* (Karlsruhe; Müller, 1955), Chapter 1.

"Nature"

Plato in *Laws* characterized "nature" as the physical system consisting of earth, air, fire, and water.[2] But he qualifies this shortly afterwards by saying that if the soul is prior to the physical system of nature, it would be the pre-eminent natural or creative power. Plato's emphasis here is clearly on creativity. Earth and air are primordially creative, but brook no comparison with the creativity and causal efficacy of the soul. Plato may have in mind his doctrine of the World Soul, as creativity "writ large."[3] as well as the individual human soul, which he is explicitly referring to.

Aristotle disassociates Nature from the Platonic World Soul, but retains the Platonic notion of a quasi-organic purposefulness in nature. Thus all natural beings, like the various organs in a physical body, act for an end, according to the patterns indicated by their substantial forms. Even the natural movements of inanimate things are "programmed" by their natural forms. Every being has something analogous to appetite, in other words basic orientations congruent to its makeup; but appetite in the strict sense is a property of animals— brute animals, which are moved towards their ends instinctively, and especially rational animals, who ideally are moved by practical reason, a rational appetite, to achieve their true end, happiness, but can be tricked by their sense appetites into seeking counterfeit happiness rather than the real thing.[4] But just what is happiness? Aristotle in his *Nicomachean Ethics* conceives the pursuit of true, long-term happiness somewhat after the manner of Hippocrates's theory of medicine—maintaining or restoring a harmony among the various "opposites." Rational or virtuous activity consists in constantly maintaining a mean between the two extremes to which our concupiscible and irascible appetites can lead us. Justice is more difficult to place in these categories—the individual virtue of justice turns out to be a mean between giving and taking in our relationships with others.[5] In our

---

[2] Plato, *Laws*, X, 891a.

[3] Plato, *Timaeus*, 34a–37c.

[4] Aristotle, *De Anima*, III, 10, 433a.

[5] Aristotle, *Nicomachean Ethics*, V, 5, 1133b. For a discussion of Aristotle's theory of virtue as a "mean," see my *Ethics in Context: Towards the Definition and Differentiation of the Morally Good* (London: Macmillan/Washington, D.C.: Georgetown University Press, 1988), 48–50.

rational pursuit of the "golden mean" and avoidance of vicious extremes, human nature becomes actualized, and flourishes.

In Stoicism, as we have seen, the emphasis was on Nature with a capital "N" as a system organized rationally by divine intelligence—a system which also extends beyond countries to the world community. Human nature as an integral part of this system is called to participate in and promote this system by rational behavior. Inclinations and appetites are discussed as part of this system by Cicero and other Stoics, but without the detailed physical analysis characteristic of Aristotle's approach.

Modern concepts of nature have been unavoidably influenced by Newtonian physics, which focused on a system of mechanics presupposing absolute space and time, non-living, and not containing any principle of movement within it. The contrast with Aristotelian physics, and Thomism, which incorporated Aristotle's scientific theories, is remarkable. The intrinsic teleology of beings functioning in accord with natural tendencies or appetites is missing. The Newtonian cosmos and bodies within it, from a strictly physical, specialized point of view, are "dead matter," which the Creator governs "not as the soul of the world, but as Lord over all."[6] The metaphor of "clockwork" is sometimes used in describing the Newtonian system. Certainly it is hard to envision organic beings within this system, except as Cartesian machine-bodies.

The word "nature" and its equivalent in many other languages, is derived from the Latin, *natus esse*—meaning to be "born" to be such-and-such with such-and-such characteristics. This emphasis on innate characteristics is found in the Aristotelian notion of nature, *phusis*, which supplied the scientific basis for Thomistic natural law and found reverberations in other subsequent natural-law theories up to the Enlightenment. In contemporary physics, in spite of the major shift in paradigms from Newtonian physics during the twentieth century, "nature" is still construed as primarily inorganic. For the most part, with the ascendancy of relativity and quantum mechanics, the focus of interest is still on the impersonal movements and interactions of matter. An interesting exception to this pattern is the resurgence of something like the idea of a "world soul" in the

---

[6] Isaac Newton, *Mathematical Principles of Natural Philosophy*, III.

guise of the "Gaia hypothesis," the "strong" version of which indicates that the world may indeed have something like an invisible life
principle.[7] Nature in this sense would be pre-eminently alive and creative, and humans would simply be participants and perpetuators of
this creativity.

As regards individual human natures, however, the torch has been
passed to the biological sciences, in which the focus at present is on
DNA molecules containing the code for the specific behavior patterns
of the human species. The classical teleological view of human nature
is thus replaced with a mechanical view: the DNA has a particular
informational structure which conditions or "programs" subsequent
developments. The DNA is also subject to mutations, the investigation of which can help to solve or confirm doubts we may have as to
the common natural endowments of all races and ethnic groups.

Mind, or reason, used to be the mainspring for the *telos* of human
nature; but now it is compartmentalized in Cartesian fashion. In the
American Philosophical Association's newsletter, *Jobs in Philosophy*,
one finds very few advertisements for specialists in the "philosophy of
human nature" or "philosophy of the human person," except in some
Catholic colleges which still maintain remnants of the Thomistic cur-
riculum; but many listings can be found for "philosophy of mind," or
related disciplines such as cognitive science and epistemology.

A contemporary update on the concept of individual human
nature would have to take into account the watersheds that have taken
place in science and philosophy. It would emphasize genetic, hereditary aspects to some extent, but focus on the mind and rationality as
essential human characteristics. Those who take exception to the
"Humpty Dumpty" split of mind from body and emotions and inclinations would want to include these neglected aspects in their analysis. Those who see "soul" as a broader and more integral concept than
"mind" would want to include not only rationality as an essential
human attribute, but also freedom, self-consciousness and possibly
social consciousness. Progress in theorizing about human nature
depends to a great extent on the relative richness of the concept of
human nature taken as the starting point.

---

[7] Rupert Sheldrake, *The Rebirth of Nature* (Rochester, Vt: Inner Traditions International, 1994).

"Natural"

"Natural" has multiple connotations, many of which are obviously not moral. The contrast of "natural" with "supernatural" does not necessarily have any moral implications. To speak about the "natural world" as different from supernatural realms, or "grace" as differing from nature, involves metaphysical rather than ethical discourse. Even "natural virtue," differentiated from "acquired virtue," is in ordinary parlance a reference to temperament or inclinations, and is at most on the pre-moral rather than the moral level. "Natural" as distinguished from "conventional" can easily have the connotation of immoral use of raw power and natural advantages, as we saw in Plato's *Gorgias*.[8] The contrast of "natural" with "artificial" often also has a morally neutral connotation. We describe computational devices as "artificial intelligence," prosthetic devices added to bodies as "artificial limbs," and products of food chemistry as "artificial sweeteners." "Artificial insemination" to replace actual sexual intercourse may have some moral implications, but these are not immediately obvious. Pope Paul VI's objections to "artificial contraception" in his encyclical letter *Humanae vitae* seem to be based not specifically on objections to artificiality (the fact that one is using man-made devices, pharmaceuticals, and so forth), but on their *unnaturality* in a stronger sense.

"Unnaturality"

"Unnaturality" in its usages seems to have connotations closer to the moral: Those who speak of the unnatural addition of heat to streams and rivers, resulting in the killing of fish and animals using the waters, may argue reasonably about the moral implications. Similarly, unnatural breaks in the ecological balance of forests, due to exploitative timbering, may lead to issues of morality. In contemporary parlance, "death from unnatural causes" often implies moral and criminal delinquency on the part of a responsible agent. Ancient traditions of binding the feet of females in China, or female circumcision in Egypt, Somalia, and elsewhere, are widely thought to be immoral. The

---

[8] See above, page 10.

Pope's restrictions regarding "artificial contraception," just mentioned, should presumably be interpreted as a disapproval of an unnatural interference with the development of embryonic human life. In terms of the Thomistic hierarchy of natural inclinations mentioned above, we could say that suicide is unnatural, as contravening the thrust towards being; that the things that we consider unnatural in animals are also unnatural in humans (for instance killing members of their own species and homosexual acts); that stubbornly remaining in ignorance about what is right and wrong is unnatural as opposed to the desire to know, and that misanthropy is unnatural as opposed to the specifically human ability and propensity to love. In the above examples, the moral elements have to do with threats or impediments to life or to serious intentional interference with normal human development. In a similar vein, one might speak of threats or impediments to freedom as both "unnatural" and immoral—for instance the unnatural restrictions of citizen movements by an authoritarian state, or the unnatural sheltering of children from the outside world by possessive or paranoid parents. To generalize, we can say that "unnatural" with a moral connotation has to do with a threat to the exercise of some essential property of human nature (or "basic value"), the right to which has not been forfeited. In other words, not just any human intervention in natural development, such as surgical bypasses and incarceration of miscreants or institutionalization of the insane is immoral; on the other hand, practices like sterilization of the retarded, imprisonment of those who offer no threat to society, institutionalization of those who are no threat to society or themselves, would fall into the unnatural-immoral category.

"Perversion"

"Perversion" is a stronger term than "unnatural," but can be used in a non-moral sense, for example eating dirt or paint chips, as a perversion of appetite; or the strange food fetishes characteristic of anorexics. But moral perversion has been described best in Plato's *Gorgias*, where Socrates rebuts Callicles, who has just asserted that even if pleasure, like an itch, requires constant scratching, it is the essence of happiness:

But suppose the itch were not confined to one's head. Must I go on with my questions? Think what you will answer, Callicles, if you are asked the questions which naturally follow. To bring the matter to a head—take the life of one who wallows in unnatural vices. Isn't that shocking and shameful and miserable?[9]

Perversion can be defined as acts or habits which are seriously unnatural, or even in a sense "against nature." Certainly extremely violent acts on fellow human beings, such as cannibalism and torture, fall into this category, as well as parent-child incest. The vomitorium in ancient Rome is frequently offered as an example of the perversion of the function of eating. (Liposuction, as a means to avoid the ill effects of gluttony, might qualify as the modern counterpart.) The term that is translated as "unnatural vices" in the above excerpt from Plato is *kinaidon*—a reference to pedophilia. St. Paul in *Romans*, as is well-known, characterizes homosexuality and lesbianism as "against nature."[10]

Freud offers a general description of sexual perversion, defining perversion in terms of the common attitude prevailing in his milieu in regard to sexual mores:

It is a characteristic common to all the perversions that in them reproduction as an aim is put aside. This is actually the criterion by which we judge whether a sexual activity is perverse—if it departs from reproduction in its aims and pursues the attainment of gratification independently. . . . [Such activity] is called by the unhonored title of "perversion" and as such is despised.[11]

Going beyond psychological descriptions to moral classifications, Aquinas characterizes masturbation, homosexuality, and bestiality as serious sexual sins—read "perversions." John Finnis writes, in a similar vein,

Some sexual acts are (as types of choice) always wrong because of an inadequate response, or direct closure, to the basic procreative value that they

---

[9] Plato, *Gorgias*, 494e.

[10] *Romans* 1:26–27.

[11] Sigmund Freud, *A General Introduction to Psychoanalysis*, Joan Riviere trans. (Garden City: Garden City Publishers, 1943), Part III, Lecture 20, 277.

put in question. By a trick of certain European languages, we call the more visibly non-procreative of these acts "unnatural."[12]

The "more visibly non-procreative" acts, in Finnis's construal, seem to be not just unnatural but perversions.

A perverse combination of violence and sex is exemplified in sado-masochistic practices—sexual satisfaction *via* the infliction or the reception of pain, glamorized in the writings of the Marquis de Sade.

What all these alleged perversions have in common is that they seem—at least to many persons—to be not just "unnatural" in a vague sense, but to be *contrary* to nature in an extreme sense. Major disagreements have arisen in recent decades regarding the inclusion of masturbation and homosexuality as perversions, or even as "unnatural"; but certainly there is broad-based consensus about the perverse nature of other practices, such as cannibalism and pederasty.

"Law"

When we speak of "law," the universal prime analogate seems to be positive law, law in the strict sense, not one of the secondary meanings. Aquinas points to civil law as the primary analogate for all law, in *ST* I–II, q. 90; other meanings are secondary. The elements in Aquinas's definition of law include proper authority, orientation towards the common good, promulgation, specification, helping to organize society, containing nothing blatantly immoral, and being subject to sanctions. John Finnis's extremely long and complex sentence defining law (here abbreviated) runs in a similar direction:

> [Law designates] rules made in accordance with regulative legal rules, by a determinate and effective authority . . . for a "complete" community, and buttressed by sanctions in accordance with the rule-guided stipulations of adjudicative institutions, this ensemble of rules and institutions being directed to reasonably resolving any of the community's co-ordination problems (and to ratifying, tolerating, regulating, or overriding co-ordination solutions from any other institutions or sources of norms) for the common good of that community. . . .[13]

---

[12] Finnis, "Natural Law and Unnatural Acts," *Heythrop Journal* 11 (1970), 385.
[13] *NLNR*, 276–77.

Finnis's remarks on the analogical use of the term, law, in the physical sciences, cited earlier,[14] deserves repeating for further analysis here:

> For our purposes, physical, chemical, biological, and psychological laws are only metaphorically laws. To say this is not to question the legitimacy of the discourse of natural scientists, for whose purposes, conversely, what we call "law strictly speaking" is only metaphorically a set of laws. The similarity between our central case [natural law] and the laws of arts and crafts and applied sciences is greater; in each case we are considering the regulation of a performance by a self-regulating performer whose own notion of what he is up to affects the course of his performance. But the differences still are systematic and significant; . . . "Natural law"—the set of principles of practical reasonableness in ordering human life and human community—is only analogically law. . . .[15]

This is an important point. We use *metaphors* when we don't have quite the right word, and decide to describe one thing in terms of another. One might have difficulty, for example, precisely describing the mathematical regularities that Newton analyzed in his laws of force and motion, and as a substitute refer to them metaphorically as "paths of nature" or "clearings in the clouds of movement" or "ingrained habits of matter" or "the balancing act of nature the juggler"—or "*laws*." The latter metaphor could be used to emphasize that gravity acts as if *commanding* acceleration for a falling body, and *prohibiting* deceleration. Similarly, if we talked about the "laws" of dynamics in sound in music, we would be indicating that sound-dynamics, like legislative rights, *allow* certain cords or sequences in major scales, but not in minor.

Analogies help to bring out a limited likeness between two things that are largely unlike, one of which is better known or more familiar. The two major types of analogies of philosophical interest are the analogy of proper proportionality and the analogy of attribution. The *analogy of proportionality* functions like a mathematical proportion, for example, $\frac{2}{4} = \frac{4}{8} = \frac{8}{16}$, but can be used to designate relationships

---

[14] See above, page 53.
[15] *NLNR*, 280.

which go beyond the mathematical. For example, a theologian trying to explain the meaning of charity might say that $\dfrac{kindness}{humans} = \dfrac{charity}{God}$; or a natural-law theorist trying to clarify the relationship of natural law to human development might draw up a law-based analogy, saying that $\dfrac{laws}{societies} = \dfrac{divine\ providence}{cosmic\ evolution} = \dfrac{natural\ laws}{human\ flourishing}$.

The *analogy of attribution,* used frequently in everyday speech, can contribute to ambiguities. When we discuss health, the prime analogate is the proper functioning of an organic body, lack of pathologies, etc.; but there are also secondary analogates not referring to organisms—healthy urine, vitamins that are healthy, rosy cheeks being a healthy sign, broccoli being supposed healthy, and so forth. Similarly, the prime analogate for law is positive law, enacted by proper authorities for a community, as mentioned above. But only by analogy can we speak of the laws of logic and, in science, Galileo's law of falling bodies, Newton's laws of gravity, Kepler's laws of planetary motion, the laws of thermodynamics, and so forth. And, as Finnis observes, the techniques and principles that artists and craftsmen follow and pass on to others, are also "laws" or "rules" only analogically.

Classical natural law theorists had more leeway than their modern counterparts. Natural law was not a secondary analogate but real law, laid down by the Creator, and accompanied by serious *sanctions.* For example, Cicero could warn that a person who breaks the laws of nature "will endure the severest penalties even if he avoid the other evils which are usually accounted punishments";[16] Locke refers to "commendation and disgrace" as the most basic sanctions backing up the natural law;[17] and Grotius, still partially anchored in the classical tradition, could observe that "injustice causes torments and anguish, such as Plato describes, in the breast of tyrants."[18]

Hobbes, distancing himself from the classical approach, was nevertheless cognizant of the strictly analogous usage in an uncharacteristic passage:

> Those which we call the laws of nature . . . are not in propriety of speech laws, as they proceed from nature. Yet, as they are delivered by God in

---

[16] Cicero, *On the Republic*, III, xxii, 216.
[17] John Locke, *An Essay Concerning Human Understanding*, II, xxviii, 12.
[18] Grotius, Prolegomena, §20.

holy Scriptures . . . they are most properly called by the name of laws. For the sacred Scripture is the speech of God commanding over all things by greatest right.[19]

Real law implies sanctions. But can a non-classical natural-law theory, priding itself on independence from any belief-system, be associated with sanctions in the strict sense, or only "sanctions" like feeling good or bad about oneself, and the like? The "laws of human nature," as Finnis and many natural-law theorists depict them, are indeed only secondary analogates. They are not really *laws* enacted by some authority, although our religious beliefs, operating in a distinct mental compartment from our moral commitments, might lead us to ascribe them to God as the source; knowledge of the existence and will of God may enhance the idea of obligatoriness, but, at least in Finnis' formulation, theological knowledge is not a necessary factor.[20] But an idea of obligatoriness without sanctions seems to be on the same level as "I really should start dieting some day to lose weight." *Sanctions* are necessary to deter individuals from serious and even heinous infractions of the law of nature, when their inclinations run in the contrary direction.

The Possibility of a Paradigm Shift

We have been presupposing that the "prime analogate" for law is positive law. But maybe the prime analogate *should* be something else— the laws of pursuit of happiness, or the law of self-preservation, or laws of loyalty or love—all other laws being merely secondary analogates. I will discuss a shift of paradigms that is conceivable, starting with an example of the "mind-body" problematic:

Discussions of the relations between mind (or soul) and body (or brain) have been beset by a major hurdle, especially since the time of Descartes. The prevailing prime analogate for *causality*, as everyone knows, is the causal relationship between two physical bodies or physical substances. Some difficulties with regard to causal explanations

---

[19] Hobbes, *De cive*, III, 33, 152.
[20] *NLNR*, 36–49.

have arisen in contemporary quantum mechanics, where probability or "stochastic" causality is relied on. But for the most part, scientists accept the "law of causality" as operative strictly on the physical level. So immense problems develop for would-be dualists, trying to explain the influence of mind on body or vice versa. If the mind is not something physical, how can it come into contact with the body that it purportedly moves, and from which it is said to receive information about its environment and positive and negative sensations? Such dilemmas impel some philosophers to try to simplify matters by removing the "myth" of the mind, and replacing it with the brain and neural network; critics like Gilbert Ryle castigate stubborn dualists as "ghost-in-the-machine" advocates; and a few recalcitrant philosophers and mystics simplify in the other direction by pointing to mind as the only reality, and bodies as mere appearance or illusion. But one could argue that the interaction between mind and body is the causal relationship that most people have the most experience of, most of the time— rational beings are constantly having influence on their bodies, and through their bodies on the physical world, and *vice versa*. Why not, then, conclude that the mind-body causal relationship is the prime analogate, and all sorts of "causal" interactions in the physical world— possibly even the obscure interactions taking place in the world of quantum physics—are mere approximations to that paradigm, mere secondary analogates?[21]

An argument with regard to natural law might follow a similar path: Possibly the prime analogate for our concept of *law* is not positive law, but the laws of our nature. These laws are expressed in the imperious and ineluctable drive to happiness, which functions as the command of all commands; likewise in the drive for self-preservation, the drive to reproduce, the drives to attain knowledge and freedom. Perhaps these are the source of our primordial experience of authoritative laws whose disobedience can put us at peril of losing ourselves. Then, when we encounter laws laid down by the municipality or the

---

[21] Others have defended the validity of the causal relationship between mind and body. See, for example, John Foster, *The Immaterial Self: A Defense of the Cartesian Dualist Conception of the Mind* (London: Routledge, 1991), especially Chapter 6. But the thought-experiment I am suggesting is something stronger. If mind-body causality were taken as the prime analogate, presumably body-body causality would be more in need of defense than mind-body causality.

state or the government, we see something analogous to the imperiousness and ineluctability of our own basic impulses. Or when we see evidence of predictable and calculable tendencies in the material world, we understand these "laws" by comparison with analogies in our experience. In other words, yes, there are also patterns and regularities "out there," in our social environment, which have claims on our attention and must be observed, just like we must heed the unwritten command within us to pursue happiness and all subordinate objectives necessarily connected with it.

Short of this shift in paradigms, and in lieu of any particular religious or theistic presuppositions, we must conclude that natural law is "law" only in the same sense that the laws of gravity and thermodynamics are laws; and that infractions of the natural law have to do partially with tendencies shared with animals, but especially with the tendencies or drives which are specific to human beings—towards freedom, knowledge, self-consciousness and social consciousness. The worst infractions of the natural law would be acts contrary to nature— the perversions. Here one would encounter a bedrock of agreement, concerning things like parent-child incest, pederasty, female genital mutilation, cannibalism, infant sacrifice, genocide, torture; but also inevitable disagreements about other *prima facie* "perversions."

6

Problem Areas in Natural Law

The Is-Ought Issue

A frequently applied metaethical standard for contemporary ethical theories is that they do not derive an "ought" from an "is." The difference between the "new" natural law theory of Finnis, Grisez, and others and the more traditional natural law theories is largely due to the assiduous efforts of the new theorists to avoid any such deduction; they consider human nature to be at most something factually existent, from which no moral values, or "oughts," can be validly inferred. The prohibition of such deductions is usually traced back to an often-cited passage from David Hume (1711–1776):

> [Morality] consists not in any *matter of fact* which can be discovered by the understanding. . . . Can there be any difficulty in proving that vice and virtue are not matters of fact, whose existence we can infer by reason? . . . [However,] in every system of morality which I have hitherto met with . . . the author proceeds for some time in the ordinary way of reasoning, and establishes the being of a God, or makes observations concerning human affairs; when of a sudden I am surpriz'd to find that, instead of . . . *Is*, and *Is* not, I meet with . . . *ought*, or an *ought not*. . . . This *ought*, or *ought not* . . . should be observ'd and explain'd . . . A reason should be given . . . how this new relation can be a deduction from others, which are entirely different from it.[1]

---

[1] David Hume, *Treatise of Human Nature*, III, i, 1.

The first thing we ought to notice from this statement is that Hume's last two sentences, with the phrases, "should be observd" and "should be given" seem to raise the question about the derivation of *these* "shoulds." Possibly they are metaethical "shoulds," concerned with norms for proper ethical argumentation, and derived from the fact of his reactions to inadequate modes of theorizing among ethicists. Also, I might be able to justify the suggestion I just made about what we "ought" to notice in this passage, by referring to the fact that there is a *prima facie* discrepancy between Hume's principle and some words used in the cited text. But, if we can set such semantic observations aside for the moment, the point Hume is making can best be understood from an examination of the context. The case Hume is using as an example in this section is the prohibition against murder. Hume challenges us:

> See if you can find that matter of fact, or real existence, which you call vice. In which-ever way you take it, you find only certain passions, motives, volitions and thoughts. There is no other matter of fact in the case. The vice entirely escapes you, as long as you consider the *object*. You never can find it, till you turn your reflection into your own breast, and find a sentiment of disapprobation, which arises in you, towards this action. Here is a matter of fact; but 'tis the object of *feeling*, not of reason. It lies in yourself, *not* in the object. The fact that we feel a strong repugnance against murder leads us to conclude that murder is wrong.[2]

The context here is all-important. Hume in the first passage above cited is arguing against a certain type of "scientific" ethical system which tries to deduce moral rules from an examination of external states of affairs. He focuses particularly on the systems of Ralph Cudworth (1617–1688) and Samuel Clarke (1675–1729),[3] which ignore the importance of feeling or sentiment, and employ reason to examine facts and relationships, thus arriving at an "abstract system of morals." This is wrongheaded, according to Hume; and in the last analysis reason with all its exertions can never produce one valid ethical conclusion in this way. But how then do we come to ethical con-

---

[2] *Ibid*. Emphasis added.
[3] David Hume, *An Enquiry Concerning the Principles of Morals*, (Indianapolis: Library of Liberal Arts, 1957), III, 2, 27n.

clusions, as, for example, that murder is wrong? In the second passage above, we see the process: we arrive at that conclusion through examining an internal fact, that is, a psychic fact—our strong repugnance for murder.

An emotivist considering these passages would very likely conclude that Hume is saying that "murder is wrong" is simply another way of saying, "I feel an abhorrence for murder!" But Hume's position is much more nuanced than this. He is not just an emotivist. He thought that the general sentiments of morality are common to all men, and that these sentiments offer the appropriate basis for valid ethical conclusions. For example, in a passage in which he is discussing the right of subjects to revolt against vicious tyrannies, he observes that the moral right in this case is not just a matter of opinion or high probability:

> The general opinion of mankind has some authority in all cases; but in this [case] of morals it is perfectly infallible. Nor is it less infallible because men cannot distinctly explain the principles on which it is founded.[4]

This is definitely not the sort of statement an emotivist would make, and shows a *prima facie* resemblance to natural-law positions. Thus Frederick Copleston portrays Hume almost as a natural-law theorist:

> [Hume's] insistence on the original constitution or fabric of human nature suggests that this nature is in some sense the foundation of morality or, in other words, that there is a natural law which is promulgated by reason apprehending human nature in its teleological and dynamic aspect.[5]

Copleston is not alone in finding an affinity between Hume and the natural law tradition. Pauline Westerman shows that Hume was operating in the context of a rather firm natural law tradition, used language and concepts from natural law, and has been interpreted by some Hume scholars as at least a "closet" natural lawyer.[6] But a bet-

---

[4] Hume, *Enquiry*, III, 2, 9.
[5] Frederick Copleston, *History of Philosophy* (Westminster, Md: Newman Press, 1959), Vol. 5, 34.
[6] Pauline Westerman, "Hume and the Natural Lawyers: A Change of Landscape," in Stewart and Wright eds., *Hume and Hume's Connexions* (University Park: Pennsylvania State University Press, 1994), 83ff.

ter explanation seems to be that he is in the *moral-sense* theory tradition, as D.D. Raphael maintains in his book on the works of
Hutcheson, Hume, Price, and Reid.[7] A moral-sense theorist concen-
trates on the area where morality and aesthetics converge, and maintains that there is a special distinct *faculty* for determining right and
wrong. Thus in the text where Hume is speaking about the repugnance for murder, he is not just speaking as an emotivist reducing
moral judgments to feelings, but as a moral-sense theorist pointing
out, in a somewhat over-optimistic way, one example of the infallible
moral sensibilities in mankind.

Hume's final summary of his position in the *Enquiry* gives a clear
indication of a moral-sense approach that Hume considered to be the
proper, reputable, empirical way to develop a scientific system of
morality:

> The hypothesis which we embrace is plain. It maintains that morality is
> determined by sentiment. It defines virtue to be *whatever mental action or
> quality gives to a spectator the pleasing sentiment of approbation;* and vice the
> contrary. . . . The ultimate ends of human actions can never, in any case, be
> accounted for by *reason*, but recommend themselves entirely to the senti-
> ments and affections of mankind without any dependence on the intellec-
> tual faculties. . . . Reason, being cool and disengaged, is no motive to
> action, and directs only the impulse received from appetite or inclination by
> showing us the means of attaining happiness or avoiding misery. . . . The
> standard of [reason], being founded on the nature of things, is eternal and
> inflexible, even by the will of the Supreme Being; the standard of [the sen-
> timents], arising from the *internal frame and constitution of animals*, is ulti-
> mately derived from that Supreme Will which bestowed on each being its
> peculiar nature and arranged the several classes and orders of existence.[8]

If we compare this with the disputed passage from Aquinas concerning the main natural inclinations[9] operating in conjunction with
practical reason, we can understand the grounds on which Copleston
likens Hume to a natural-law theorist. But it would be more accurate

---

[7] D. Daiches Raphael, *The Moral Sense* (Oxford, 1947); see also James Q. Wilson, *The
Moral Sense* (New York: The Free Press, 1993).

[8] *Enquiry Concerning the Principles of Morals*, Appendix 1, "Concerning Moral
Sentiment" (emphasis added).

[9] See above, page 20.

to say that Hume advocates a *conjunction of reason and sentiment* in making moral decisions: reason, to investigate the facts and relations and determine utility (Hume was a proto-utilitarian); sentiment to bring humans to final judgments about right and wrong. In other words, he was objecting against those (metaphysicians *et al*) who would try to arrive directly at moral judgments by logical analysis and abstract reasoning, without any consideration of human inclinations. He almost seems to be conducting a pre-emptive attack on Finnis! To paraphrase, he is saying "bring your moral sense to bear on the facts uncovered by reason, and this is the way to arrive at reliable moral decisions."

Thus Hume's interdiction of deriving an "ought" from an "is" is directed at those who would want to use reason, which is competent only to determine the truth and falsity of external facts, to arrive at moral principles or rules. But as he states, regarding the example of our repugnance for murder, "here is a matter of fact; but 'tis the object of *feeling*, not of reason." In Hume's estimation our "oughts" can indeed be reliably engendered by internal sentiments, common to the majority of humankind, registering our reactions to the states of affairs that reason recognizes as existing.

It should be noted, however, that a deduction from sentiments has major limitations. It envisages feelings or inclinations that have definite moral bearings. Thus it is irrelevant to challenge someone following Humean principles to deduce an ought from our feelings of pride or ambition or competitiveness, or our need for human sympathy or property. But we could deduce an ought from our feeling of sympathy for others, our repugnance for injustices, our drive for self-preservation, our desire to nurture our children, and the like.

The misinterpretation of Hume on this point, and the considerable opposition to deriving an "is" from an "ought," may not just be a matter of textual difficulties or philosophical conundrums. Philip Devine suggests that "those who reject the claims of the Is to determine the Ought work within a metanarrative in which humanity is seen as progressively freeing itself from the bonds of nature.[10] Max Black suggests that there are cultural aspects (including philosophy as a subculture) which may make it necessary to keep "is" and "ought"

---

[10] Philip Devine, *Natural Law Ethics* (Westport: Greenwood Press, 2000), 55.

absolutely distinct. He states that moderns endorse what he calls "Hume's guillotine" because first of all, there is a widespread belief that "no term may occur in the conclusion of a valid argument unless it occurs, or can be made to occur by suitable definitions, somewhere in the premises."[11] Secondly, he feels that many moderns believe that ought-statements make no truth claims at all, "and are therefore disqualified to serve either as premises or as conclusions."[12] In a similar vein, Alasdair MacIntyre points to a basic inconsistency in the way that modern logicians, who have a more favorable view of induction than Hume, nevertheless reject Hume's arguments against induction. Modern logicians reject what he has said about induction (Hume assumes that all arguments must be deductive, or else defective), but it is an outmoded neo-Humean skepticism that prevents *us* from getting an "ought" from an "is."[13] Hume himself uses the term, "deduction" in the classical passages discussed above; but a modern logician, more sanguine about induction, might find it not inconsistent to justify an inductive process, if deduction seems out of the question.

G.W.F. Hegel (1770–1831) opposed Kant's post-Humean and non-Humean insistence that morality should have no relationship to natural inclinations, as if reason could simply make moral decisions by a purely rational procedure. Hegel argues that this would be a strange sort of morality indeed:

> The "cancellation" of inclinations and drives can't be taken seriously; since it is just these inclinations and drives that constitute *self-actualizing self-consciousness*. Moreover, they should not be *repressed*; rather, they should merely be *conformable* to Reason. They are indeed conformable to Reason because moral *action* is nothing but consciousness actualizing itself, thereby giving to itself the configuration of a "drive."[14]

In other words, practical reason has to join forces with natural inclinations in order to make any moral choices and engage in any

---

[11] Max Black, "The Gap between 'Is' and 'Should'," in *The Is-Ought Question*, [1] Hudson (Macmillan: London, 1969), 101–02.

[12] Black, 102.

[13] A.C. MacIntyre, "Hume on 'Is' and 'Ought'," in *The Is-Ought Question*, 35–50.

[14] G.W.F. Hegel, *Selections from Hegel's Phenomenology of Spirit: Bilingual Edition with Commentary*, translated and annotated by Howard P. Kainz (University Park: Pennsylvania State University Press, 1994), §622.

moral activity. This is one of the few areas where one might find a convergence of viewpoints between Hume and Hegel.

It must be admitted, however, that this viewpoint entails a certain optimism about human nature. A philosopher who considers human nature as a bundle of selfish and malicious drives that need to be repressed or politically regulated would have *a priori* obstacles to accepting the more sanguine viewpoint just discussed. The key to understanding Hume and Hegel seems to lie in the coordination of reason with the inclinations or sentiments. The selfish or malicious drives are by definition, the ones where coordination with reason is absent or deficient.

The Fact-Value Distinction

In twentieth-century ethics, the fact-value distinction is often used—like the "falsifiability" criterion in the philosophy of science—as an initial "litmus test" for determining the potential viability of an ethical theory. The fact-value distinction is wider than the is-ought distinction, since "value" can have aesthetic, political, and religious, as well as ethical, connotations. But it is most often used with regard to ethics; and in this domain of discourse, it goes beyond the largely logical proscription of "deriving an ought from an is" to a metaphysical proscription of confusing the objective realm of facts with the presumably subjective realm of values. Thus a person who objects to deriving oughts from ises need not necessarily hold to a sacrosanct separation of facts from values. He or she might hold that there are some facts which are also values, such that no derivation is necessary; or that there are certain morally significant things that many people would not characterize as "facts" but are nevertheless factual, such as emotions or inclinations. Such a person would run afoul of the fact-value distinction, but not necessarily of the ought-from-is proscription.

With regard to the fact-value distinction, we should notice first of all that the distinction that is actually, factually made between fact and value, is a major, current value in metaethics; and that the factual prohibition of disregarding this distinction is considered a valuable directive for furthering progress in ethical theory. In other words, even in making the distinction it is difficult to find language which does not relativize the alleged sharp division between facts and values. On the other hand, the *source* of the distinction, and its long-lasting power, is clear. It is an offshoot of the classical Cartesian distinction between non-extended thinking minds and extended material substances, *res cogitans* distinguished from *res extensa*, subjectivity from objectivity; and Ralph McInerny adds that the distinction receives a particular and ongoing impetus from the Kantian emphasis on the autonomy of practical reason (the proper province of values) from theoretical reason.[15] Descartes, aware of the problems connected with his theory, tried to find a connection between mind and brain in the pineal gland, and post-Cartesians such as Spinoza and Leibniz tried to bridge the gap between thought and being in their own systems; the German idealists, Fichte, Schelling, and Hegel, concerned more specifically with the Kantian dichotomies, made similar efforts in the nineteenth century; Whitehead, the later Wittgenstein, and others in the twentieth century have also been concerned with bridging the gap. But the problematic is still with us, especially in ethics. Natural-law theory is particularly susceptible to criticism, especially if the "nature" referred to with the adjective "natural" is considered to be something factual in which certain moral values are allegedly imbedded or implicated.

The fact-value distinction is easier to discern with some kinds of facts than with others. If I say "the book is on the table," I may get fairly broad agreement that this is a mere fact—although it may be necessary to avoid considerations such as what value I personally place on "sticking to the facts," or what values I connect with properly organizing my home office, or the values I attach to finally finding the lost book which I had been searching for, or to being able to point out a book that I fully agree with and would secretly like my onlookers to read. But the distinction becomes unwieldy and shows symptoms of untenability when I speak about "democracy" or "classical art," and try to distinguish the factual elements from the elements of value. The problem, of course, is with hybrids. In ethics a particular problem emerges with the issue of emotions, for which the presence of subjectivity is a *sine qua non*, but which are also physical, measurable by changes in blood pressure, pulse, nerve

---

[15] See Ralph McInerny, *Aquinas on Human Action: A Theory of Practice* (Washington, D.C: Catholic University of America Press, 1992), 118.

reactions, and the like. It would presumably take a degree of sophistication in instrumentation not presently attainable, perhaps unattainable, to distinguish with any accuracy the factual aspects of emotions from the subjective aspects.

In natural-law theory, the main "fact" which seems to be of crucial importance is the pursuit of happiness, or the goal of "human flourishing." One would be hard-pressed to *derive* any values from this "fact," since it is already intrinsically value-laden. We can mentally separate the desire or the drive, and refer to it as an empirical phenomenon; but it would be hard to deny that it is at the same time the fundamental, originary source of value, possibly all value, very probably moral values. What conclusions could a natural-law theory draw from this realization? A "soft" version of natural law may simply concern itself with indicating and elaborating ways of achieving human flourishing; a "hard" version, supplemented with the corollary of a divine legislator, might go beyond this to determine obligations, duties, prohibitions, and sanctions related to, or connected with, this drive. Versions between these two extremes are, of course, also conceivable.

The "Naturalistic Fallacy"

Classical natural-law theories, which unabashedly strive to make connections of morality with nature or human nature, have been apt candidates for accusations of committing the "naturalistic fallacy," as it was called by G.E. Moore. According to Moore, utilitarians like Jeremy Bentham and J.S. Mill do a disservice to ethics by setting up some natural good as their normative criterion—in the case of Bentham and Mill the maximization of pleasure quantitatively or qualitatively for as many people as possible. Regarding the natural "goods" thus attained, we can always ask, "but is it (or are they) good?" The naturalistic fallacy consists in defining good in terms of any of the various kinds of goods—moral, aesthetic, functional, and so on—that can be associated with it. All of these associations are subject to the "open question" test—"but is *x* good?"—which can always be subjected to doubt, since *x* is not a synonym of "good." To maintain that saying "*x* is good" is the same as saying "good is good" is to fall into the naturalistic fallacy.

As even sympathetic proponents have pointed out,[16] the naturalistic fallacy could have been more accurately named, since it is neither naturalistic (it would also apply to non-natural properties associated by metaphysicians with good) nor fallacious (it does not involve an invalid inference, but rather an unwarranted definition). Less sympathetic proponents[17] have argued that the naturalistic fallacy is not only misnamed but irrelevant, and that Moore himself is inconsistent in first characterizing good as indefinable but then offering several definitions for good, such as "intrinsic value," "intrinsic worth," or that which "ought to exist."[18] In spite of doubts about the nonfallaciousness of the naturalistic fallacy, and widespread inability to intuit good as simple and indefinable in Moorean fashion, most would-be ethical theorists understandably want to avoid being conceptual bedfellows with J.S. Mill, Herbert Spencer, the sociobiologists, and others tempted to reduce morality to the pursuit of some evolutionary, social, or psychosocial objective. And it does seem *prima facie* that for natural-law theory, in many of its reformulations, good is connected with, if not reduced to, some sort of conformity to nature. So this merits further investigation.

One major difference that we find in comparing even classical natural-law theories with consequentialist and utilitarian theories is the fact that while, for the latter, moral goodness is achieved by pursuing non-moral goods—such as maximization of pleasure for the majority—for natural law the pursuit is for goods which are not morally indifferent—self-preservation, practical reasonableness, and so forth. As we have seen in Chapter 5, various interpretations of "nature" and "natural" are possible. But if we test a natural-law theorist with Moore's "open question"—for example, "Is conformity to nature good?" or "Is avoidance of what is contrary to nature good?"—it is not inconceivable that the theorist could answer "yes" without blinking, and present a credible answer for his affirmative response. Likewise, while the question would have to be phrased in very general terms, the answer would always be in terms of moral good, thus

---

[16] See for instance Julian Dodd and Suzanne Stern-Gillet, "The Is-Ought Gap, the Fact-Value Distinction, and the Naturalistic Fallacy," *Dialogue* 39 (1995), 740.
[17] For example Bernard Baumrin, "Is There a Naturalistic Fallacy?" *American Philosophical Quarterly* 5 (1968) 79ff.
[18] Baumrin, 88.

falling short of the very wide parameters of good in the Moorean formulation, encompassing non-moral connotations.

Aristotle uses a quasi-Moorean "open question" technique at the beginning of his *Nicomachean Ethics*, examining the various desires that humans have—for pleasure, for wealth, for beauty, and so forth—and asking over and over again, "but is this sought for its own sake, or for the sake of something else?" And Aristotle, after quite a few negatives, does come up with a "yes" answer, something that is sought for its own sake—*eudaimonia*, roughly translated as "happiness." If Moore asked whether this was good, we along with Aristotle—as long as we had in mind the good that is humanly attainable in this life (and not some Platonic ideal good, that is, the transcendent Idea of Good) —could conceivably maintain that there is no difference between asking "is happiness good?" and asking "is good good?"

Teleology

Regarding the "big picture," Teleology with a capital "T", major metaphysical problems exist in our day. Alfred Russel Wallace, the co-discoverer with Darwin of evolutionary natural selection, was a life-long proponent of a teleological interpretation of evolution, involving special creation of humans by spiritual forces.[19] But the Darwinistic interpretation of evolution, which eschews teleological explanations, has prevailed. Darwinism tells us that the human race is the result of chance developments taking place over billions of years; and contemporary physics often portrays the development of the universe as a similar progression of chance developments after a primordial Big Bang (which may itself have been the chance offshoot of developments in other universes!). It is much more challenging now than in previous eras to defend Cicero's observation that "the entire universe is regulated by the power of the immortal Gods; . . . by their nature, reason, energy, mind, divinity, or some other word of clearer signification, if there be such, all things are governed and directed."[20] The "strong anthropic principle," favored by Harvard chemist Lawrence

---

[19] See Michael Shermer, *In Darwin's Shadow: The Life and Science of Alfred Russel Wallace* (Oxford: Oxford University Press, 2002), 226–232.

[20] Cicero, *On the Laws* ["Marcus" speaking in the dialogue], I, vii, 407.

Henderson and British astrophysicist Fred Hoyle, offers a teleological interpretation of the universe, leading Hoyle, who did not believe in a personal God, to admit that "his atheism was shaken." [21] But this is a minority position. A current challenge for metaphysics is to find an underlying rationale for purposefulness amid what sometimes seems to be an ocean of chance occurrences.

Fortunately, problems that may exist with regard to cosmic Teleology do not necessarily cast doubt on teleology with a small "t". As Larry Arnhart points out,[22] even if modern physics seems to deny teleology, modern biology does not. Modern biologists must explain animate nature as serving certain ends. The growth of plants and animals to maturity, for example, or the striving of animals to satisfy their needs, implies natural ends or goals that become part of any full biological explanation. A similar distinction is relevant regarding human ethical development: Aristotle, for example, even though he was philosophizing in the context of a physics accepting eternal cosmic cycles of rotating spheres, was able to develop an ethics based on a linear progression towards the only concrete good sought for its own sake— happiness. Thomistic natural-law ethics presupposes a similar *telos*, with the addendum of divine providence operating behind the scenes in human affairs.

In modern ethics, we are confronted with branchings-out of disparate interpretations of teleology. In Kant's Newtonian universe, characterized by reliable mechanistic movements in absolute space and time, teleology in ethics became etherialized as a focus upon the human person as an end in himself, giving rise to Kant's "second formulation" of his Categorical Imperative (*"treat humanity . . . in every case as an end withal, never as means only"*).[23] In contemporary metaethics, the label, "teleological," has been rather arbitrarily given to utilitarianism and other consequentialist ethical approaches, which do not necessarily subscribe to the existence of purposefulness in any

---

[21] John Barrow and Frank Tipler, *The Anthropic Cosmological Principle* (New York: Oxford University Press, 1988), 21–22; Timothy Ferris, *The Whole Shebang* (New York: Simon and Schuster, 1997), 305.
[22] Larry Arnhart, "Aristotle, Darwin, and Natural Right" in *Darwinian Natural Right: The Biological Ethics of Human Nature*, (New York: State University of New York Press,1998), Chapter 1.
[23] Kant, *Fundamental Principles*, 45–46.

strong sense in human development, and very often leave questions about the rationale or obligatoriness of consequence-oriented activity unanswered. Other ethical theories not dubbed teleological are nevertheless teleological in their main thrust. Karl Marx's master plan of revolution presupposed the teleological thrust of social evolution toward replacing oppressive bourgeois "morality" with a new type of socialist consiousness or conscience. Nietzsche's counter-revolution against socialist homogenization envisaged an inexorable movement of the "will to power" toward the production of at least one value-creating individual *Übermensch*. In more recent times sociobiologists tell us that many moral values result from the way we have been "programmed" to maximize advantages for our genes.

Even if we grant, for argument's sake, that evolution, including the evolution of humans, has been ruled by chance interactions with the environment, purposeful development of organisms is still meaningful. There is no need to "throw out the baby with the bathwater." An acorn, for example, or a caterpillar, may have developed purely by chance from prior species; but the unfolding of the organism into an oak or a butterfly still has a definite finality with a determinate number of stages attached to it. We can "bracket out" the more formidable metaphysical questions about cosmic teleology. There is an important teleology relevant to individual animal organisms; we can make judgments about their mature state, and we can make valid judgments at certain stages as to what should be or not be the case.

So also, with humans: we know that the mature state to which humans can aspire involves certain ontological and biological perfections, and especially certain perfections of consciousness which are attainable only by the human species; and we can make valid judgments about what should or should not take place in the course of human development. A hierarchy of functions is not irrelevant. For example, the drive toward reproduction could be superseded to facilitate rational goals; the self-preservation instinct could be countermanded in favor of saving the life of another. Unfortunately questions about obligatoriness and sanctions still remain! The assertion of natural teleology does not of itself entail any warnings about what will happen if we ignore it. But we can validly discuss "tendencies" and "basic functions" and the ends to which they lead.

The concept of maturity, then, or what Finnis calls "human flourishing," is derived from what we know about the natural unfolding of humans, with special attention to the qualities that make human beings distinctive—self-consciousness, social consciousness, the cultivation of talents, the pursuit of maximal freedom, and so forth. To come up with a valid list of things essentially connected with the mature state of humans thus seems to require attention to the teleological development of the human organism, best clarified by a strategic bracketing-out of metaphysical issues concerning teleology in the universe.

Law and Sanctions

If murder, theft, and perjury are infractions of the natural law, they are also prohibited by positive laws in most cultures, but with a variety of interpretations and a variety of sanctions. The legal sanctions prevalent in some cultures for adultery, sodomy, incest, defamation of character, and child-neglect may also be related in the mind of the legislators to their conception of the natural law. But it is a truism that many or most of the flagrantly immoral acts go unpunished, leading to considerable cynicism about purported rewards for virtue. As Kant observed,

> The sight of a being who is not adorned with a single feature of a pure and good will, enjoying unbroken prosperity, can never give pleasure to an impartial rational spectator. . . . There arises in many, if they are candid enough to confess it, a certain degree of misology, that is, hatred of reason. . . . They end by envying rather than despising the more common stamp of men who keep closer to the guidance of mere instinct, and do not allow their reason much influence on their conduct.[24]

G.W.F. Hegel, commenting on this remark, accuses Kant himself of a very subtle kind of immorality—jealousy of evildoers blessed with all kinds of good fortune, while virtuous persons are often plagued with difficulties and sufferings.[25] But jealousy aside, it would seem that even to an impartial observer, a natural law that had no concomitant sanctions would be a very weak candidate indeed for the

---

[24] *Ibid.*, 11–13.
[25] G.W.F. Hegel, *Selections*, §625

appellation of "law." Recognizing this, most traditional theorists have bolstered their natural law or laws with appropriate sanctions.

For Cicero, the main sanction is what might be called a sense of alienation from oneself, and general internal distress—the sort of phenomenon that Kant's jealous observing moralist, focusing just on the externals, would miss:

> He who does not obey [the law of nature] flies from himself, and does violence to the very nature of man. And by so doing he will endure the severest penalties even if he avoid the other evils which are usually accounted punishments.[26]

According to Locke, social approbation is the most powerful sanction for morality, and social disapprobation the strongest disincentive:

> He who imagines commendation and disgrace not to be strong motives on men to accommodate themselves to the opinions and rules of those with whom they converse seems little skilled in the nature or history of mankind; the greatest part whereof he shall find to govern themselves chiefly, if not solely, by this law of fashion.[27]

Grotius emphasizes internal distress as a sanction even for lawbreakers who avoid civil punishments:

> Law, even though without a sanction, is not entirely void of effect. For justice brings peace of conscience, while injustice causes torments and anguish, such as Plato describes, in the breast of tyrants.[28]

Pufendorf, like Dmitri in Dostoevsky's *The Brothers Karamozov*, looks to religion, with its *other*worldly sanctions, as the indispensible bulwark against wanton individual and social degredation:

> In natural liberty, if you do away with fear of the Deity, as soon as anyone has confidence in his own strength, he will inflict whatever he wishes on those weaker than himself, and treat goodness, shame and good faith as

---

[26] Cicero, *On the Republic*, III, xxii, 360.
[27] John Locke, *An Essay Concerning Human Understanding*, II, xxviii, 12
[28] Grotius, *Prolegomena*, §20

empty words; and will have no other motive to do right than the sense of his own weakness. The internal cohesion of states also would be perpetually insecure if religion were abolished. . . .[29]

Aside from religious faith, there is no way to ascertain the existence of rewards or punishment in the afterlife. But there does seem to be some empirical confirmation of sanctions involving internal distress as a result of antisocial or criminal activity. The extremely sophisticated polygraph instruments used by the F.B.I. and other investigative agencies, examining changes in blood pressure, heart-beat, change in color of complexion, brain waves, galvanic skin response, and other physiological signs, show a high degree of accuracy, although they are not foolproof. The person who is "living a lie" would likely fail a polygraph test, if the pertinent questions were asked. An actor has to take on an alien persona for a few hours; but the hypocrite who must constantly hide and dissemble will almost certainly experience psychological and possibly also physical distress. One thinks of the double-agent, the life-long adulterer who has to hide his other life from wife and family, the priest or minister who preaches one thing to his congregation and does another thing in his private life.

On the other hand, it would seem that at least some people would not suffer, simply because they have never experienced the satisfaction from living morally; they are in a state of self-satisfaction, with nothing to compare it to—for example, the "hit man," with no compunction, no conscience, only thoughts of loyalty to the gang; the pathological liar who really believes his lies and has no concern about consistency. In general, anyone who has never risen to what Kierkegaard called the "ethical stage" of existence would have a natural immunity to feelings of guilt or self-doubt. The natural law for them would portend no sanctions, at least in the present life, and would thus not be recognized as a *bona fide* law.

The Problem of "The One and the Many" Revisited

In ancient philosophy metaphysical questions arose about the relationship between unity and multiplicity in general, but special attention was given to this problem also in regard to discussions of virtue

---

[29] Pufendorf, *On the Duty of Man and Citizen*, I, 4, 43

(or virtues). This ancient philosophizing seems quaint by the standards of contemporary "virtue ethics," but may be relevant to our investigation of the existence and characteristics of natural law. In the next section, we will examine the various types of natural law—natural law *stricto sensu*, the empirical natural law, and analogical natural law. But in whatever domain of discourse we choose, the question inevitably arises: should we be looking for a single general law, or multiple equipotent laws, or multiple laws in a hierarchical order, perhaps specifying one overarching law to which other laws are subordinated? The ancient discussion may provide us with some models for further progress on these questions:

In Plato's *Protagoras*, Socrates poses the following question about the virtues to his interlocutor, Protagoras:

> Are wisdom and temperance and courage and justice and holiness five names of the same thing? Or has each of the names a separate underlying essence and corresponding thing having a peculiar function, no one of them being like any other of them?[30]

Protagoras responds that all the virtues except courage have some similarities, but courage could exist in a person who is "utterly unrighteous, unholy, intemperate, ignorant." Socrates then examines the issue of courage, and gets Protagoras to admit that only the person knowledgeable about dangers has courage as distinguished from rashness or rage. The tentative conclusion seems to be that courage, and *a fortiori* other virtues, cannot exist as isolated functions of the psyche, but at least require knowledge. (Socrates remarks ironically toward the end of this dialogue that, in indicating the necessity of knowledge for virtue, he seems to have reversed a position he took earlier that virtue cannot be taught.)

In the *Republic*, Plato goes further than in the *Protagoras* with the examination of the problem, and points to justice as a unifying virtue, which harmonizes the other three virtues of [practical] wisdom, temperance and courage:

> The just man . . . sets in order his own inner life, and is his own master and his own law, and at peace with himself; and when he has bound

---

[30] Plato, *Protagoras*, 349a.

together the three principles within him, which may be compared to the higher, lower and middle notes of the scale, and the intermediate intervals—when he has bound all these together, and is no longer many, but has become one entirely temperate and perfectly adjusted nature, then he proceeds to act, . . . always thinking and calling that which preserves and co-operates with this harmonious condition, just and good action, and the knowledge which presides over it, wisdom. . . ."[31]

"Meta-virtue" is probably the best description of justice, as Plato conceptualizes it; justice is a virtue that harmonizes the other virtues. Note the relationship of this position with the issue raised above, about sanctions: the sanction for the unjust person would be to exist in disharmony, and any semblance of temperance, courage, and wisdom observed in this person would be pseudo-virtues because of their lack of inner coordination.

Aristotle in the *Nicomachean Ethics* answered the question about the unity versus diversity of the virtues differently, designating prudence as the primary virtue, and assigning a hierarchical hegemony of prudence over the other three moral virtues, temperance, fortitude, and fairness; for Aristotle, prudence is the one "virtue of virtues."

John Finnis in a sense seems to be doing something Aristotelian: In Finnis's theory of natural law, "practical reasonableness," in the domain of the basic values, seems to be the hierarchical chief virtue, or supreme moral law. At the very least, practical reasonableness seems to be the "first among equals." Finnis, however, does not assign it any hierarchical precedence.

For Plato and Aristotle and Finnis, one can use a variation of Moore's "open question" test, and ask, "why be just," "why become prudent?" or "why be practically reasonable?" Only Aristotle addresses a version of the "open question," as mentioned above; and his answer would obviously be in terms of happiness or fulfillment, since we can't ask "why pursue happiness?" while we can ask that question about every other pursuit, including the pursuit of prudence. Thus in Aristotle's formulation, if there is one overarching natural law, leading to all subsidiary moral directives, and instigating the attainment of virtue, it would seem to be the pursuit of happiness or fulfillment, broadly defined as Aristotle defined it. But Aristotle himself

---

[31] Plato, *Republic* IV, 443e.

does not place this in the category of a "natural law." And it would not be best characterized as a virtue or even a meta-virtue, but as a necessary, although not sufficient, cause of virtue.

Secular *versus* Religious Versions of Natural Law

The first explicitly religious version of natural law is certainly to be found in the letter of St. Paul to the Romans, where Paul, using metaphors redolent of the prosecution and the defense in a court of law, compares the law given by God to the Jews with the unwritten law applicable to the gentiles:

> Pagans who never heard of the Law but are led by reason to do what the Law commands, may not actually "possess" the Law, but they can be said to "be" the Law. They can point to the substance of the Law engraved on their hearts—they can call a witness, that is, their own conscience—they have accusation and defense, that is, their own inner mental dialogue . . . on the day when, according to the Good News I preach, God, through Jesus Christ, judges the secrets of mankind. . . . You [Jews] preach against stealing, yet you steal; you forbid adultery, yet you commit adultery. . . . By boasting about the Law and then disobeying it, you bring God into contempt.[32]

Paul may have been familiar with, and influenced by, Stoic notions of natural law.[33] In the passage just cited, Paul is pointing to the last seven commandments of the Decalogue given to Moses as embodying the same law that pagans are led to by reason (thus indicating that there is a strictly secular version of these commandments). In proto-ecumenical fashion, he indicates that the Last Judgment will have to do with conformity to this law in the heart, regardless of whether the observance was connected with religious orthodoxy. The natural law thus apparently becomes the great equalizer between

---

[32] *Romans* 2:14–16, 21–24.

[33] See Michael Crowe, *The Changing Profile of the Natural Law* (The Hague: Nijhoff, 1977), 54–56; and James Barr, *Biblical Faith and Natural Theology: The Gifford Lectures for 1991, Delivered in the University of Edinburgh* (Oxford: Clarendon, 1993), 21ff.

secular and religious persons, in the last analysis. You might say that this is "the bottom line" in Paul's doctrine of salvation.

Obviously many of the classical theories we have discussed, from Cicero to Aquinas and Pufendorf, have at least implicit religious or theistic moorings. These theories maintain their credibility as philosophical or ethical theories by taking reason as their starting point. The existence of God and notions of divine law are either inferred with concomitant metaphysical arguments, or taken for granted as a faith commitment complementing the ethical system.

A strictly secular natural-law theory would need to assert independence from faith commitments and also from a theistically-oriented metaphysics. Although Hobbes refers obliquely to the possibility of connecting natural law with the divine,[34] it is generally held that he was not speaking out of any personal religious or philosophical convictions.[35] Grotius tried to keep his empirically-oriented theory independent of Christian commitments, but is less than persuasive when he asserts the validity of his theory on a purely scientific basis. Finnis's analytical approach recognizes the added weight that metaphysical and religious presuppositions could give to his theory, but is concerned with developing a theory that will be acceptable to all and only those who can follow him on a strictly rational level, *sans* appeal to emotions or inclinations.

An atheistic natural-law theory would be considered a contradiction-in-terms to many traditional theorists. But it is not inconceivable that a passion for science or the analyses of practical reasoning, coupled with purely secular interpretations of "nature" and "law," could lead an atheist to a strong defense of natural law. For example, the journalist, Nat Hentoff, a self-proclaimed atheist, has opposed abortion on the basis of what could be called a natural-law principle—the unbroken continuum of life from conception.[36]

---

[34] See above, page 65.
[35] For challenges to the "received" view, see Francis Hood, *The Divine Politics of Thomas Hobbes: An Interpretation of Leviathan* (Oxford: Clarendon, 1964), 229, 234–36; and Aloysius Martinich, who maintains, in *The Two Gods of Leviathan: Thomas Hobbes on Religion and Politics* (New York: Cambridge University Press, 1992), that Hobbes was a committed and orthodox Christian.
[36] See Nat Hentoff, "There's More to Abortion than Abortion," in Theresa Wagner, ed., *Back to the Drawing Board: The Future of the Pro-Life Movement* (South Bend: St. Augustine's Press, 2003), 217.

The Challenge of Slavery

This is a problem only for those who believe that the natural law applies to all times and places, and that slavery is one of the most obvious infractions of the natural law. Presuming that most, or at least a large number, of people throughout the ages, including some of the most intelligent persons in history, were upright in intentions and in conformity with what we consider to be the basic tenets of the natural law, how could they be so mistaken as to support slavery? What seems self-evident to us was apparently not, to them. Aristotle condoned slavery for "natural slaves," including many non-Greeks;[37] St. Paul in his epistle, *Philemon*, exhorts a slave master to be kind to a runaway slave converted to Christianity and returned by Paul to his master; Aquinas, following Aristotle, allows slavery in cases where it will be "useful for someone to be ruled by a wiser person";[38] Grotius waffles regarding slavery, approving its legitimation by Aristotle and St. Paul, but also finds the institution of slavery objectionable;[39] Pufendorf has no problem with slavery, and seems to think that many or most slaves have become enslaved through free choice, as a means of subsistence.[40] But any modern natural-law theorist from any of the major "camps" would classify slavery as abominable and vicious. This apparent change in position leads Van den Haag to observe that natural law is prone to subjectivism and capriciousness:

> Just as some philosophers inferred from natural law that slavery is wrong, others, particularly in antiquity (Aristotle among them), found that slavery is justified by natural law.[41]

In a similar vein, Carl Henry observes that

> Natural law theorists—reaching back to and before the pre-Socratics— have themselves at times disagreed over the precise content of natural

---

[37] Aristotle, *Politics* I, 6, 1225b, 4–15.
[38] *ST*, II^aII^ae q. 57, a.3, ad 2, 59.
[39] Grotius, *De Jure Belli ac Pacis*, I, Chapter 3, viii, §1; II, Chapter 22, xi; III, Chapter 7, vi, 5; III, Chapter 14, viii.
[40] Pufendorf, *On the Duty of Man and Citizen*, II, 4, §§1ff., 129.
[41] Ernest Van den Haag, "Not above the Law," *National Review* 43 (1991) 35–36.

law. It has been invoked to defend freedom and slavery, hierarchy and equality.[42]

Certainly the variety of positions regarding slavery has been a major source of cynicism about natural law. A partial solution to this cynicism lies with the concept of freedom, which has undergone such extraordinary vicissitudes in history. Except in Sartrean existentialism, freedom is a right, not a duty. The natural law corresponding to this right would be the duty to respect the freedom of others, or at least not to jeopardize it, aside from cases such as criminality and self-defense. In any case, there was hardly any recognition of the right of freedom in our sense of the word in the ancient and even in the medieval worlds. There were other senses of freedom: Hereditary rights in monarchies and aristocracies; citizen rights in Athens; property rights in Roman law; Christian freedom, as escape from the slavery of sin; freedom interpreted by some of the stoics, as indifference to external setbacks and oppression; Buddhist freedom from desire, and hence freedom from suffering.

The list could be continued. But the main point is that the modern concept of individual freedom and the multiplicity of rights associated with it is the result of a cultural and intellectual evolution that has taken place over the last few centuries in many parts of the world, in tandem with the ascendancy of democratic political institutions. Aristotle and Plato, highly critical of the Greek experiments with democracy they were familiar with, had no concept of inalienable individual rights inhering in everyman.[43] The philosopher Epictetus, though himself a freed slave, exhorted his followers to rise to a state of stoical intellectual freedom which could be attained by a slave as well as by an emperor. The jurist Ulpian thought that slavery belonged in

---

[42] Carl Henry, "Natural Law and a Nihilistic Culture," *First Things* (January 1995), 55–60.

[43] Fred Miller, Jr., in *Nature, Justice, and Rights in Aristotle's* Politics (Oxford: Clarendon, 1995), 108–09, argues that although there is a problem translating our notion of "natural rights" into Aristotle's Greek, Aristotle himself was aware that "wise men" in his milieu defended notions of individual rights. Miller concludes, "It is unfortunate that Aristotle does not go further and concur with ancient Greek thinkers such as Alcidamus and Philemon who seem to imply that there could be no right by nature to own a slave."

the category of the *jus gentium* rather than the *jus naturale*. Aquinas, influenced by Aristotle's politics and anthropology, considered slavery to be a subsidiary development, along with the institution of private property, added to the natural law of social organization, but not a practice directly connected with the natural law. Both Suarez and Grotius, like Ulpian, ascribed slavery to the "law of nations."

No doubt the "law of nations" in the sense of a common denominator of legal customs in the nations of the world is still a viable concept today; but with modern democratic developments in the understanding of natural rights, slavery can no longer be legal anywhere. In the twentieth century, slavery was still legal in many countries, until legalized slavery was finally abolished during the seventies. Recurrences of slavery still continue, however, in various parts of the world; and practices such as child labor, sweatshop labor, and prison labor can amount to virtual slavery.

The situations in which slavery was formerly justified or condoned in connection with natural law seem, in retrospect, to be attributable to a lack of coordination of the *jus naturale* with a theory of natural rights. The important issue of the interrelationship of natural rights and natural law will be considered in the next chapter.

7

Types and Classifications of Natural Law

As explained in Chapter 5,[1] difficulties in interpretation of natural law arise from the fact that most natural law theories, for example that of Aquinas,[2] take positive law, which requires an actual lawgiver or legislators, as the prime analogate. But others distance themselves from this requirement, with theories that are about "law" only in an analogous or metaphorical sense. The various types of natural law can thus be differentiated, depending on whether 1) a divine lawgiver is presupposed, or 2) a sum-total of human legislators, or 3) in a purely analogous way like the "laws" of science.

The first type is natural law *stricto sensu*, a real law with a real lawgiver; the lawgiver may be God as arrived at by natural reasoning, as for the Stoics, or the God of revelation, as is the case for many Christian natural-law theorists. The second type is akin to one version of what has been traditionally called the "law of nations"—an empirical analysis of the main moral principles backed up by law in all cultures, on the supposition that at least these must offer us a bedrock of pivotal universal and unchangeable precepts. The third type, recognizing that scientific laws have largely unquestioned authority in spite of the absence of any actual "lawgiver," is modeled on the various analogous senses in which we can speak of scientific theories, hypotheses, or principles as "laws."

---

[1] See above, page 62.
[2] *ST*, 1ª2ᵃᵉ, q. 90.

Natural Law in the Strict Sense

The paradigmatic example of natural law in the strict sense with a Lawgiver, promulgated for the common good, ordering relationships among members of the community, based on nature itself, is the Decalogue entrusted to Moses in the Hebrew Bible (Cf. *Exodus* 20:2–17; *Deuteronomy* 5:6–21). St. Paul in *Romans*[3] compares the "natural" observance of the Ten Commandments by many "pagans" with the non-observance by many Jews, who boast about having the revealed "law." The examples Paul gives in *Romans* have to do with laws regarding killing and adultery and idolatry, but the other commands of the Decalogue are implicitly included. Consulting the Catholic and Protestant concordances[4] on interpretation of the commandments, and taking into account the different numbering systems for the Decalogue, we find the following points of agreement regarding the main prohibitions of the revealed natural law:

- *Specifically religious stipulations:* Idol-worship, hexing, and black magic were prohibited; and the uniquely Hebraic institution of a Sabbath day was inculcated.

- *Neglect of the elderly:* "Honor thy father and mother" does not seem to refer primarily to young children, but to adult offspring, who were obligated by this commandment to care for a parent in their old age, usually the mother after the father had died. Intuitively, we notice that good people in every culture do this; Confucianism probably emphasizes familial obligations more strongly than any other religion or ethic.

- *Killing:* By "thou shalt not kill" intentional, premeditated killing is meant, with some exceptions; the killing of animals, execution of criminals, and killing of enemies in war is not prohibited.

- *Adultery:* "Thou shalt not commit adultery" was not only a moral injunction, but a capital offense, both for the guilty

---

[3] See above, page 87.
[4] Raymond Brown *et al.*, *The New Jerome Biblical Commentary* (Englewood Cliffs: Prentice Hall, 1990); and Charles M. Laymon, ed., *The Interpreter's One-Volume Commentary on the Bible* (Nashville: Abingdon, 1971).

woman and the guilty man, although enforcement for males was lax. Sexual intercourse with someone engaged to be married was also prohibited. Such restrictions would also help assure *bona fide* certainty of progeny for the male—to avoid what sociobiologists characterize as being "cuckolded"—tricked into raising the offspring of someone else.

- *Perjury.* The eighth commandment was meant to prohibit the defamation of character, which could result in undeserved death for the victim of perjury—for instance someone accused of adultery. Honesty in official statements and contractual commitments seemed to be also implied.

- *Stealing.* Scripture scholars point out that the word translated as "stealing" was commonly used to refer to kidnaping or selling into slavery. But stealing in the more usual sense is indicated in the later commandment about not coveting "your neighbor's goods."

Concerning these precepts of the Decalogue, we should notice first their *wide scope.* In the commandments related to interpersonal relationships, the ultimate boundaries, not to be trespassed, consist of acts such as murder, breaking contracts, contempt for elders, theft and robbery, and marital infidelity. But the prohibition of killing does not encompass less drastic injuries to life; the prohibition of adultery does not explicitly encompass simple fornication or homosexuality. Suarez,

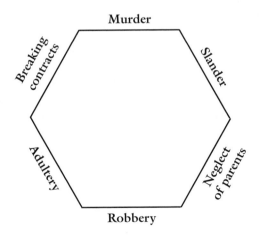

as we have seen,[5] argued that a process of reflection is necessary for us to see that other precepts, both positive and negative, are entailed in the decalogue.

Aside from extensive reflections, we see that the explicit commandments are few and all negative except for the commands to observe the Sabbath and to honor parents. Like Socrates, who claimed in his trial[6] that his *daimon* "voice" only warned him if he was entering into a potentially evil direction, but never interfered with his choices among goods, the Decalogue seems to be saying, "do whatever you like, but steer clear of these morally pernicious boundaries." We might presume that many, if not most people, whatever their religion or non-religiousness, will be able to avoid these outer boundaries. Presumably the further one stays from these outer limits, and gravitates towards the center, the better off he or she will be morally. The vows taken in religious orders and monastic communities—such as poverty and chastity—seem to be motivated by this consideration—leading to Aquinas's defense of the withdrawal of monks or religious from the temptations of the world, in order to have an easier time of achieving salvation![7]

It should be noted, however, that amid the largely negative duties enjoined by the Decalogue, a number of basic rights are implied. The prohibition of killing implies a right to life. The last few commandments imply the right to property (wife and children and slaves would seem to be included as a type of property). The rights to freedom and personal dignity, which are uppermost in the mind of moderns, don't receive even implicit recognition at this early stage in the development of social consciousness.

But it is too easily forgotten that the overarching duty which sums up all the commandments is love. In the Hebrew Bible, not only is love for fellow Israelites enjoined—"You must love your neighbour as yourself" (*Leviticus* 19:18)—but also for "aliens": "If a stranger lives with you in your land, do not molest him. You must count him as one of your own countrymen and love him as yourself—for you were once strangers yourselves in Egypt."[8] In the New Testament this com-

---

[5] See above, p. 26.
[6] See Plato's *Apology*, 31d.
[7] *ST*, 1ª2ᵃᵉ q. 184, a.8, ad 6.
[8] *Leviticus*, 19:34.

mandment of love is characterized by Jesus as the "greatest commandment," as summing up in one phrase "the whole law and the prophets."[9]

Is a natural law based on love conceivable? No major theories have gone in that direction, although one could argue that love is just as important as rationality, among human capacities. John McDermott's discussion of this possibility is suggestive:

> The task of natural law theorists manifests itself: to preserve and strengthen the natural human signs of love in marriage, family, friendship, and all natural institutions while guaranteeing life and liberty as love's necessary presuppositions.[10]

The Empirical Natural Law

To many denizens of contemporary culture who hear of the natural-law search for principles applicable to all times and all places, it must seem that the obvious way to conduct this search would be through sociological and anthropological data, or the development of a political consensus such as led to the development of the Universal Declaration of Human Rights approved by signatories of the United Nations Organization.

Following such empirical approaches, we would presumably end up with the ultimate "opinion poll." If it could be shown that the same basic obligations are recognized and revered (even if not consistently adhered to) in *every* culture and race and ethnic group, this would seem to avoid cultural relativism. Rather than "morals are dictated by your culture," the lesson would be "all cultures agree on a certain bedrock of moral rules."

Grotius favored this approach, distinguishing the *a priori*, normative method of "demonstrating the necessary agreement or disagreement of anything with a rational and social nature" from the *a posteriori*, empirical method of "concluding, if not with absolute assurance, at least with every probability, that that is according to the law of nature which is believed to be such among all nations, or among all

---

[9] *Matthew*, 22:36–40.
[10] John M. McDermott, S.J., "Love and the Natural Law," *Vera Lex* 9 (1989), 12.

those that are more advanced in civilization."[11] Grotius would have been delighted to have access to the extensive empirical data now available, and might have discarded the *a priori* approach entirely in favor of such studies. For example, Donald Brown's exhaustive analysis of human "universals" in the cultures of the world includes moral universals—such as rules of personal responsibility and hospitality, and the prohibition of murder, rape, incest, and child-abandonment—which would bolster an empirically-based "global" natural law theory.[12]

Eberhard Schockenhoff also considers as significant the list of "potential moral universals" drawn up by Klaus Peter Rippe in his study of ethnographic literature:

> This core sector includes both obligations *vis-à-vis* one's relatives (sexual taboos, the rejection of adultery, the precept of exogamous marriage, reciprocal obligations between parents and children, solidarity *vis-à-vis* one's progeny, an obligation to regulate inheritance) and obligations of solidarity in relation to society as a whole (readiness to cooperate within the group, care for the poor and disadvantaged, duty to obey the leaders). Within the clan of one's relatives, one's own society, or human society as a whole, there exists a universal acknowledgment of the prohibition of murder and lying, the condemnation of rape and of deliberate aggression in general, the duty of *pietas* to the dead, the precept that promises must be kept, and a universal obligation to mutual help which goes beyond cultural boundaries. As well as these moral precepts which regulate personal attitudes, expectations of loyalty, and obligations of solidarity among individuals, we also find social-ethical obligations derived from the various economic parameters of existence (regulations concerning property, prohibition of theft, ideas concerning justice).[13]

Kant, in contrast, put a damper on the pursuit of an empirical natural law, indicating that any results it achieved would be deficient in the *obligatoriness* we associate with moral rules:

---

[11] Grotius, I, i, xii, §1.

[12] See Donald E. Brown, *Human Universals* (Philadelphia: Temple University Press, 1991).

[13] Eberhard Schockenhoff, *Natural Law and Human Dignity: Universal Ethics in an Historical World* (Washington, D.C.: Catholic University of America Press, 2003). The reference is to Rippe's *Ethischer Relativismus: Seine Grenzen, seine Geltung* (Paderborn: Schöningh, 1993), 110–12.

The basis of obligation must not be sought in the nature of man, or in the circumstances in the world in which he is placed, but *a priori* simply in the conception of pure reason; and although any other precept which is founded on principles of mere experience may be in certain respects universal, yet in as far as it rests even in the least degree on an empirical basis, perhaps only as to a motive, such a precept, while it may be a practical rule, can never be called a moral law.[14]

Kant in this passage is pointing out the important distinction between a descriptive and a normative ethics. But if the empirical findings about moral values become, for all practical purposes, worldwide, cannot this maximal quantitative augmentation boost the findings qualitatively, to the higher status of normativity and obligatoriness?

Contemporary ethicists commonly warn about the pitfalls of doing a merely "descriptive" ethics that can have no prescriptive or normative significance. There are some exceptions, however. Phillip Ekka suggests that an empirical survey of diverse cultures is not irrelevant to a normative natural law. Ekka, in his analysis of primitive societies, concludes with the following generalizations: there is universal condemnation of incest; polygyny and to a much lesser extent, polyandry, exist along with monogamy, in societies stricken by war and other calamities; promiscuity is sometimes permitted, if it does not result in offspring; murder, especially intratribal is prohibited.[15]

If an extensive empirical examination of cross-cultural moral values were successful in disclosing certain constants, perhaps backed up by historical records that indicate constancy over the centuries, what conclusions could be drawn from this? According to Grotius, there are two alternatives.

When many at different times, and in different places, affirm the same thing as certain, that ought to be referred to a universal cause; and this cause, in the lines of inquiry which we are following, must be either a correct conclusion drawn from the principles of nature, or common consent. The former points to the law of nature; the latter, to the law of nations.[16]

---

[14] Kant, *Fundamental Principles*, 5.
[15] Philip Ekka, S.J., "Anthropology and the Idea of a Universal Moral Law for Society," in Illtud Evans, O.P., ed., *Light on the Natural Law* (Baltimore: Helicon, 1965), 120ff.
[16] Grotius, *Prolegomena*, §40.

In other words, a widespread effect like this requires some explanation through some cause or causes. Grotius points to two possible
interpretations. The preferred explanation depends to a significant
degree on one's attitude towards human nature. One who believes in
a uniform human nature will find such phenomena corroborative of
that belief, providing possibly even an empirical test of the validity of
moral principles deduced from an analysis of human nature. It is possible also that one who was skeptical about a uniform human nature
on *empirical* grounds—because of evidence of endless cultural diversity—would be instigated by such facts to re-examine his or her position concerning human nature. But even if one's skeptical position
regarding human nature remained unchanged, he or she could
bracket out considerations about human nature, and accept the findings of universal consensus as evidence of a "law of nations."

Whatever the interpretation, a successful proof of a cluster of basic
moral values by an empirically-based natural law would seem to offer
us an interesting convergence of fact and value—the factual existence
throughout the globe of certain moral norms. These moral norms, on
a first-order level (not from the point of view of a natural-law theorist
or metaethics), would not be derived from the facts nor would the
facts be in any way separate from the values. The values would simply
be imbedded in the facts. This essential intertwining would stand as a
"limiting case," at least one exception to the rule of fact-value sepa-
rateness. From the vantage point of *descriptive* ethics, it would be
superfluous to ask, "are these values in fact valuable?" Whether or not
the moral values thus ascertained would be considered *normative* and
obligatory for individuals, would depend on the degree of commitment of individuals to the multiplicity of legislators presupposed for
the enactments of the "law of nations." This would involve a considerable extension of the concept of the "law-abiding citizen."

Natural Law by Analogy
(An Expansion on a Theme of Finnis)

As was discussed in Chapter 5,[17] natural law can be considered "law"
by analogy, like scientific laws such as Galileo's law of falling bodies,

---

[17] See above, page 63.

Boyle's law, the chemical law of constant proportions, Mendel's laws of heredity, and so forth. Admittedly, scientists are cautious in using the term "law," reserving this title for theories that have been so thoroughly used and tested that they are no longer considered just "hypotheses." Thus Alan Guth's "inflation" theory for explaining the origin of galaxies in the universe has been widely accepted in the last two decades, but is not yet referred to as a law; and the Darwinian theory of "natural selection," although almost universally accepted by biologists, is not considered a law. Sometimes political or ideological motivations lead advocates to promote theories prematurely to laws, such as the "law of the survival of the fittest," "the law of diminishing returns," and the "law of increasing returns." But designations as "law" in science are characteristically reserved to operational hypotheses that have weathered the storms of scientific revisions and attained to classical or semi-classical status.

If we pursue this analogy one step further, we find that scientific laws are not monolithic, but can be further subdivided according to their characteristics. Three possible subdivisions (this is not meant to be an exhaustive classification) include 1) *tendencies*—such as gravity, as it appears to us earth dwellers, as a downward force, although in the "big picture" of relativity, it is much more complex than this; or (possibly a better example) the second law of thermodynamics (entropy), which predicts a unidirectional movement of energy to less and less usable forms; 2) *interactions* involving mathematical relationships between variables or constants, such as Newton's laws of motion or his inverse-square law of gravity, or Einstein's revised conservation law, $e = mc^2$; and 3) *polarities* involving complementary opposition, for example the "laws" of electricity and magnetism resulting from Maxwell's equations or Lenz's Law.

The rationale for characterizing scientific tendencies, interactions and polarities as "laws" is, as I argued in Chapter 5,[18] based on the similarities they bear to the characteristic of actual laws—in a sense, they seem to control physical phenomena, they are responsible for a certain regularity or predictability in nature, they can bring about states of harmonious equilibrium or homeostasis in many situations, and there are both positive and negative consequences connected

---

[18] See above, page 63.

with our acting in harmony with the laws (for instance knowing how to close an electrical circuit safely, not jumping from too high a perch).

But analogies to law in the strict sense can also be found in the aspects and operations of human nature:

1. Natural Laws as Tendencies

A. SELF-PRESERVATION

In common parlance, people speak of the "law of self-preservation," and can depend on a quasi-intuitive understanding of the meaning of that phrase. Discussions about our duty to defend our rights, to care for our health, to avoid situations of danger, and so forth, have as their "common denominator" this tendency or law. Aquinas, as we noted,[19] applied this law more widely, ontologically, to a universal appetite to stay in existence, shared by rocks and trees, as well as animals and people. On the basis of its intuitive clarity, this principle has a good chance of receiving widespread consensus: but the difficulty is in working out the details! Suzanne Uniacke's article, "Self-Defense and Natural Law,"[20] offers us a good example of the complexity of working out principles of self-defense, even if one is committed to the principle of self-preservation. In order to justify self-defense on the basis of the law of self-preservation, we must demonstrate that there is a real need for defense, that we the defenders are not intentionally or unintentionally guilty of complicity for bringing about the situation we are defending ourselves against, that we are not causing unwarranted harm to innocent bystanders or other affected parties by our defensive actions, and so on. But aside from the difficulties of applying the basic principles to contingent cases, the "law" itself seems quite clear and unambiguous and applicable to many situations. If it is able to escape the challenges posed by the "naturalistic fallacy,"[21] it may serve as a paradigm of the type of natural law engen-

---

[19] See above, page 21.
[20] Suzanne Uniacke, "Self Defense and the Natural Law," *American Journal of Jurisprudence* 36 (1991), 73–101.
[21] See above, pages 77ff.

dered empirically by the proclivities of human nature. The success of Hobbes's theory of the "state of nature"[22] as well as H.L.A. Hart's widely respected emphasis on survival as the only admissible natural law[23] seems to provide additional testimony about the intuitive acceptability of the law of self-preservation.

B. PRESERVATION OF THE SPECIES

The tendency toward "reproduction" possessed by humans in common with animals[24] implies, in the narrow sense, begetting children, but even by Aquinas is applied more widely to the nurturance and education of progeny. The rationale for this is the fact that humans cannot attain mature independent existence without many years of such care. Their situation is in sharp contrast with that of many animals which can move, feed themselves, and develop on their own shortly after birth. In a sense, a baby is just a potential human being; physical birth lays the groundwork for a longer process of gestation which ordinarily ends at adolescence, and is overseen by biological parents or their surrogates. Contemporary studies of children growing to physical maturity without human interaction, for example the "feral children," offer us empirical confirmation of the essentially social nature of humans—if such confirmation were needed. One *law* connected with the impulse to reproduction might be designated the "law of sexual responsibility." In contemporary culture this phrase has taken on extraneous meanings such as using condoms before sexual intercourse or not contributing to overpopulation; but in its fundamental meaning it simply implies assuming responsibility for nurturance and education of any children resulting from voluntary sexual congress. This is arguably the most basic application of the natural law relevant to sexuality.

For those influenced by the Hebrew Bible, sexual responsibility has taken on the stronger connotation of the command to "increase and multiply and fill the earth."[25] In the Christian tradition the force of this command has been mollified, to admit of exceptions like vol-

---

[22] See above, page 34.
[23] See above page 44.
[24] See page 20.
[25] *Genesis* 1:28

untary celibacy, and especially in Catholicism the command has become construed negatively—rather than "have children," it reads "don't interfere with reproductive processes by artificial contraception." The papal encyclical *Humanae vitae*[26] cites Thomistic natural-law principles as the source for this conclusion; but Finnis, although departing from traditional Thomistic interpretations comes to a similar conclusion:

> What, in the last analysis, makes sense of the conditions of the marital enterprise, its stability and exclusiveness, is not the worthy and delightful sentiments of love and affection which invite one to marry, but the desire for and demands of a *procreative* community, a family. Some sexual acts are (as types of choice) always wrong because of an inadequate response, or direct closure, to the basic procreative value that they put in question.[27]

This has to be read in the context of arguments going on during the 1960s in the aftermath of *Humanae vitae* as to whether the love or unity aspect of sexuality wasn't equally as important or even more important than reproduction. But a distinction can be made between sexuality as a natural tendency shared with animals, and as interconnected with the love of a rational being. From a teleological point of view, as a natural tendency sexuality always and intrinsically is oriented towards reproduction, while only intermittently connected with love, depending on human intentions. Consistent with this basic position, Finnis also finds homosexual acts as "morally of a kind" with contraceptive acts.[28] These cogitations illustrate the fact that the position one takes regarding contraception has wider ramifications than appear at first analysis of the issue. For instance, if contraception is allowed for married couples, why not for any couples, at least where there are strong affective ties? And if affection be not an essential element of ethical sexual union, what sexual act short of inflicting violence can be interdicted?

In other words, the mental disconnection of sexuality with reproduction can have far-reaching cultural implications. Some might con-

---

[26] Pope Paul VI, *On the Regulation of Birth* (Washington, D.C.: United States Catholic Conference, 1968)
[27] Finnis, "Natural Law and Unnatural Acts," *Heythrop Journal* 11 (1970), 383, 385.
[28] *Ibid.*, 385.

sider sexual acts morally neutral, recreational activities that can be engaged in at will, as long as no one is harmed. Some others, in view of the "overpopulation" problem, would consider the increase in contraceptive devices and acts a boon to contemporary civilization, almost as if the natural law concerning reproduction should be currently reformulated as a duty or mandate *not* to reproduce, or to sharply curtail the number of one's offspring. Others would see the ethical issue about reproduction in the context of a conflict with another "natural law"—the law of preserving the environment, in particular the demographic environment.

Anxieties about the increase of world population are largely variations on the Malthusian theory—Thomas Malthus's eighteenth-century prediction that population would increase exponentially while food supplies increased arithmetically. This theory was one of the major inspirations for Charles Darwin in his development of the theory of natural selection, but unlike Darwinism it has not weathered the tests of time. Although the Malthusian theory is still cited by some as scientifically valid, its predictions have been falsified, since food supply has been shown to increase in tandem with population increases.[29] In fact, in many European countries, the population "explosion" has become an implosion, moving from "zero population growth" to negative growth.

The myth of non-exponential increase of food supplies is often combined with the myth of lack of space. But if the present world population of around 6.1 billion could be transplanted to the state of Texas with 7.3 trillion square feet in area, each person would have about 1,200 square feet to himself or herself. This is not to argue that there is no overpopulation problem, but only to indicate that what we

---

[29] See Colin Clark, *Population Growth: The Advantages* (Santa Ana: Sassone, 1972); Nick Eberstadt, "Population and Economic Growth," *Wilson Quarterly* 10:5 (Winter 1986); Peter T. Bauer, *Development Frontier: Essays in Applied Economics* (Cambridge, Massachusetts: Harvard University Press, 1991); Julian Simon, *Hoodwinking the Nation* (New Brunswick: Transaction, 1999); Ronald Bailey, "The Law of Increasing Returns," *The National Interest* 59 (Spring 2000); Anthony Trewavas, "Malthus Foiled Again and Again," *Nature* (8th August, 2002). Some economists emphasize the fact that ideas and technology are major elements which must be factored into any deliberation concerning the satisfaction of material needs. See for instance P. Romer and R. Nelson, "Science, Economic Growth, and Public Policy," in Bruce Smith *et al.*, *Technology, R&D, and the Economy* (Washington, D.C.: Brookings Institution, 1996).

call the overpopulation problem is not a *Lebensraum* problem; it is a problem of too many *poor* people. And a technical approach like contraception cannot solve the problem. If modern contraceptive methods were promoted and implemented worldwide, the numbers of poor people might be reduced, along with the numbers of the rich; but the *percentage* of poor people—due to lack of support from extended families, increased exploitation of a diminishing workforce by employers, increased industrial and agricultural unemployment, lack of governmental provisions for social security, etc.—could easily increase rather than decrease. In other words, if there is a viable application of natural law relative to the overpopulation problem, it would seem to pertain not to the issue of reproduction, but rather to issues of sociality or natural distributive justice, which will be discussed below.

Aside from the question of the proper interpretation of "overpopulation," however, it is clear that a natural law which considers the preservation of the human species as a fundamental principle will necessarily lead to important ecological questions—the care of the earth, combating pollution, preparing the environment for future generations. Such questions, not contemplated by classical and even many modern natural-law theorists, have become unavoidable and paramount in the contemporary world with its breathtaking advances in industrialization and technology.

In recent years sociobiology, with its theory about the "selfish gene" that leads individuals to altruistic and even self-sacrificing acts in order to preserve one's genes, has concluded to *descriptive* rather than normative values concerned with preserving the life and promoting the welfare of one's kin, especially one's children and siblings. Questions about ecological responsibilities and about responsibilities to future generations would also be within the parameters of sociobiological theory. But the drive to preserve the human species and the earthly environment can be taken one step further—interpreted not just as an interesting and empirically demonstrable facet of human behavior, but as a norm inviting rational assent and cooperation.

C. SPECIFICALLY HUMAN TENDENCIES

If there are any tendencies which have normative implications for humans, these will be the species-specific tendencies not shared with any other beings. Here we come to a long-standing question in philosophical anthropology: if there is a difference-in-kind (not just a difference-in-degree) of humans from the other animals, what is it? About this, opinions differ. Rationality is the most often cited distinguishing characteristic. Certainly self-consciousness, social consciousness, and freedom as the power of self-determination, are important, if not defining, human characteristics. The following is an expansion of some natural-law implications connected with these tendencies:

Rationality. Even most ethicists who do not accept natural-law connections will agree that morality consists in acting rationally. But "rationality" is an umbrella term that has multiple connotations. For purposes of clarity, it will help to explore these differing connotations and their possible implications separately.

Rationality, of course, can be *theoretical* as well as practical. In its theoretical aspect, it is concerned with pursuit of the truth, and the avoidance of ignorance. The natural curiosity of children and the desire to learn can and should evolve into steady, if not dedicated, attempts to know the truth. But it is clear that this tendency is often thwarted or diverted by passions, environmental pressures, religious or political commitments, and so forth. Aberrations connected specifically with this tendency involve intentionally closing off one's mind from certain types of knowledge—leading to ideology, liberal or conservative, leftist or rightist, carefully avoiding any contact with viewpoints differing from one's own set opinions; bigotry, being unwilling to hear good and constructive things about members of a despised race, ethnic group, religion or nationality; or misology, a strange and unnatural hatred of reasoning, deliberation and argument, seen as major threats to personal happiness.

In the practical realm, rationality both in ordinary speech and in philosophical discourse is often connected with *consistency*, the choice of actions based on principles, and the avoidance of self-contradictions. Self-consistency, insofar as it avoids self-contradictory exceptions made on behalf of one's own selfish interests, leads to universalizable maxims, to use Kantian terminology. Kant's first formulation of the categorical imperative (*"Act only on that maxim whereby thou canst at the same time will that it should become a universal law."*[30]) indeed

---

[30] Kant, 38

offers us a paramount example of the equation of rational consistency with moral validity, and the universalizability that results from applying tests for consistency. "Good Reasons" theories as a class also emphasize consistency, although with a less systematic methodology than that found in Kant's categorical imperative. One could also argue that Finnis in his efforts to establish the self-evidence of his "basic values" is in effect testing them for their inherent self-consistency.

But rationality has other important meanings: The *proportioning of means to ends*—often involving, for humans, conceptualized goals in the distant future, and often a willingness to completely abandon habitual or traditional means when other means turn out to be more suited to chosen ends. However, granted that one's ends are moral, the moral imperatives turn out to be chiefly negative rather than positive. In other words, choosing the right means is a matter of prudence, but questions about morality arise concerning the use of wrong means ("the ends justifies the means" syndrome), or, as Kant puts it in the second formulation of the categorical imperative, choosing what can *never* be a mere means to your ends, namely another person. Likewise, the "principle of double effect" allows evil or deleterious effects as the result of a choice only if the negatives are unintended and unavoidable concomitants and the goal is moral and necessary; the principle reads, "do *not* choose even good goals unless these conditions are satisfied."

Although classical ethical theories are almost unanimous regarding the importance of rationality for morality, they add to the above list even more, variant definitions of rationality. For Aristotle, rationality consisted in the *golden mean*, choosing a mean between two extremes—temperance as a mean between overindulgence and insensibility, courage as a mean between foolhardiness and cowardice, etc. In Adam Smith's *Theory of Moral Sentiments*, and other "objective observer" theories, the rational person is the one who can put himself in another's place and become an *impartial observer* of his own actions or behavior. In Spinoza's *Ethics*, rational behavior is a process of *sublimation*, starting with the *conatus* or basic impulse to perfection, by which we transform raw passions or emotions into more and more refined rational behaviors.

Self-determination: Freedom, or self-determination, as an essential aspect of human nature, is traditionally portrayed as a bulwark against various unethical character traits—conformism, slavery to the passions, remissness in developing one's talents, and so on. Plato in his *Gorgias* devises the Gyges-ring test to distinguish a pseudo-morality of convenience or fear, from real morality. He suggests a thought-experiment—imagining we have a magic ring to make us invisible, and then considering whether we would still adhere to our moral values. If we falter in this thought experiment, we show that these values are not freely chosen, and thus we are not really moral. Jean-Paul Sartre, opposed to Freudian psychoanalysis and the notion that a person's problematic actions can be blamed on the "unconscious," emphasizes the obligation of recognizing one's freedom and manifesting it, taking full responsibility for all one's actions. For Sartre, recognition of one's own freedom becomes the fundamental standard for morality.

Social consciousness. Certainly utilitarianism, making the otherwise inexplicable transition from individual happiness to social welfare and well-being, finds justification for this in human and humane tendencies of fellow-feeling. With some allowance for a great difference of contexts, Kant's principle of a "kingdom of ends"—the vision of a world community of self-legislating and self-coordinating moral agents—can find its justification in a similar fashion, although Kant himself characterizes this principle as an achievement of pure practical reason.

D. CONVERGENCES OF FACT AND VALUE, RIGHTS AND DUTIES

All the above tendencies involve a dovetailing of fact and value, "is" and "ought." Self-preservation is both a factual drive dramatically marshaled in situations of danger or assault, and a fundamental value continually applied for the maintenance of personal health, welfare, safety, and sanity. The preservation of the species, likewise, is an imperious drive most evident in familial relationships, as well as a value inculcating continual concerns for future generations. The distinctively human desire to progress in knowledge, freedom and communal relationships is likewise an indubitable fact and a cherished value requiring cultivation by society at large.

In these same primary tendencies there is also a dovetailing of rights and duties, illustrated by civil laws in most cultures. The right of all citizens to life, freedom and association with others, the right of children to nurturance and education, is guaranteed in various ways in many cultures, with statutory punishments for those who infringe on these rights. Civil laws will also enforce the duty of parents or care-takers to nurture and, in various degrees depending on the sophisti-cation of the culture, educate their children; and the duty of adults to perform various civic duties. The duty to preserve one's life, since it pertains to the individual and is not subject to public scrutiny, seems to offer a possible exception; but police or other public authorities will often intervene to prevent suicides or self-destructive behavior.

2. Natural Laws as Interactions

Pursuing the analogy to scientific laws, we look for the moral equiva-lents to e = mc^2, F=MA, and the like. The most obvious candidate as an "interactive" moral law would have to be the Golden Rule,[31] which certainly qualifies as an ethical theory in which there is a sys-tematic attempt to coordinate variables. Here the "variables" are your expectations from others and their expectations from you. Aquinas characterizes the Golden Rule as a more explicit specification of the commandment of love: it tells us *how* to "love our neighbor as our-selves."[32] Many contemporary ethicists consider this "grandfather of all ethical theories" to be complementary to a "good reasons" approach in ethics, insofar as it spells out concretely how to maintain rational consistency in one's relationships with others.

Kant's diffidence about the viability and value of the Golden rule is based primarily on the fact that, unlike his first formulation of the categorical imperative, it does not touch on any duties to oneself:

> Let it not be thought that the common: *quod tibi non vis fieri, etc.,* ["what you do not want others to do to you, etc..."] could serve here as the rule or principle. For it is only a deduction from [the Categorical Imperative], though with several limitations; it cannot be a universal law, for it does not contain the principle of duties to oneself, nor of the duties of benevolence to others (for many a one would gladly consent that oth-ers should not benefit him, provided only that he might be excused from showing benevolence to them), nor finally that of duties of strict obliga-

---

[31] *Matthew* 7:12; *Luke* 6:31; *Tobit* 4:15.
[32] *ST,* 1ª2ᵃᵉ q. 99, a. 1, ad 3

tion to one another, for on this principle the criminal might argue against the judge who punishes him, and so on.[33]

Kant's objection regarding the omission of duties-to-oneself would be applicable to many natural-law theories and, indeed, many ethical theories, which focus primarily on relations with others, and only secondarily, if at all, on relations with oneself. But it is not necessary that an ethical theory should envisage all possible relationships. It seems clear that the Golden Rule pertains only to social interactions; but this fact should not be interpreted as indicating that self-relationships are not an ethical issue. As Kant observes, "duties of benevolence" are not envisaged by the negative version of the Golden Rule which he cites, but they can be enjoined by the positive version, "act towards others as you would wish them to act towards you." The situation of judge *vs.* criminal that Kant refers to, is outside the parameters of the Golden Rule, since a criminal by his crime has forfeited some civil rights.

Sidgwick's objection is more relevant. In the *Methods of Ethics*, he says: "[The Golden Rule] is obviously unprecise in statement; for one might wish for another's co-operation in sin, and be willing to reciprocate it."[34] In other words, it could do damage in the hands of an unscrupulous literalist. This is a bona fide problem, but not insuperable. The proper utilization of the Golden Rule requires that those who invoke it be on the *ethical level*, and also that it be related to the determination of *rights*. Otherwise, it becomes an ethically neutral or perverse type of "game theory," suited to help an individual get at least as much as he gives, or be reciprocated for any kind of services or favors. As applied to rights, it can be reformulated: "If you have certain rights, be willing to grant these same rights to others in comparable situations."

3. Natural-Law Polarities

Finally, laws in science sometimes consist of bipolar relationships—between north and south poles, positive and negative electrical polar-

---

[33] Kant, *Fundamental Principles*, 47n.
[34] *The Methods of Ethics* (London: Macmillan, 1963), 379–380.

ity, and so on. Moral counterparts to such laws exist. They can be considered on an individual or a social level.

The most intuitively clear and widely recognized polarity within the *individual* consists of a polarity between the ideal self and the real or empirical self. Psychologists speak of the "level of aspiration" which must be maintained neither too high nor too low, to enable dynamic personality development—an excessively low level of aspiration leading to buried talents and stagnation, and an excessively high level leading to unrealistic goal-formation, with discouragement and/or guilt resulting when these goals are inevitably not met. The ethical state, according to Kierkegaard,[35] consists in the "task" of coordinating these two, the ideal self and real self. We could argue, with Kierkegaard, that this is the primordial ought, the Ought with a capital "O"—namely, that we ought to *have* "oughts." Kierkegaard calls this "entering the ethical stage." Our continuance in the ethical stage then consists not only in keeping our real self in line with our ideal self, but also in maintaining this dynamic tension between ideal and real self.

In the *social* dimension, the main polarity is between rights and duties, and the ethical imperative in the objective sphere, as Hegel indicates,[36] consists in a coordination of rights and duties. Our concentration in this book is on the theoretical foundations of natural law, not on natural right. But it is interesting that, whereas there is continual debate about the existence of natural law or laws, there seems to be a widespread consensus about natural rights, as indicated by the Universal Declaration of Human Rights approved by member states of the United Nations.

The 1948 Charter of the U.N. includes rights to life, liberty, and security of person, equality before the law, privacy, marriage and parenthood, the right to own property, freedom of thought, conscience, and religion, as well as the right to work, the right to education, protection against unemployment, enjoyment of the arts, and many other rights in the legal, political, and cultural spheres. The fact that there are no serious challenges to this list of rights may be an indication of a certain claim to self-evidence which it possesses, so that attempts at proof

---

[35] See Kierkegaard's *Either/Or*, trans. Walter Lowrie (New York: Anchor, 1959),Volume 2, 263.

[36] See G.W.F. Hegel, *The Philosophy of Right*, trans. T.M. Knox (New York: Oxford University Press, 1967), §§129–141.

would be superfluous. Possibly we can start with this *consensus* itself, and the fact that rights and duties are at least partially correlative; i.e., a right implies certain corresponding duties, although a duty (if duties to oneself are admitted) does not necessarily imply a corresponding right. And if, as seems likely, "human rights" include many "natural rights" not recognized by the U.N. or by the positive law of member states, certain concomitant natural laws may be generated from the list on the basis of the right-duty polarity. Certainly the rights to life, property and liberty would be included toward the head of such a list of human/natural rights, and some obvious correspondences suggest themselves (at least in a very general way, before the inevitable exceptions and qualifications are brought up).

The coordination of rights and duties with regard to *life* is clearly and eloquently expressed in Albert Schweitzer's primordial moral principle, the "reverence for life":

> The elemental fact, present in our consciousness every moment of our existences, is: I am life that wills to live, in the midst of life that wills to live. The mysterious fact of my will to live is that I feel a mandate to behave with sympathetic concern toward all the wills to live which exist side by side with my own. The essence of Goodness is: Preserve life, promote life, help life to achieve its highest destiny. The essence of Evil is: Destroy life, harm life, hamper the development of life. The fundamental principle of ethics, then, is reverence for life.[37]

Application of this principle on the national and international level will lead to tough questions about the use of resources in distributing welfare, helping poor nations, etc. But on the basic individual level, it comes down to the conclusion that we have a duty to respect the life of anyone who has not forfeited the right to life. The question about who forfeits the right to life, and how it is forfeited, is subject to differences of opinion, as is evidenced by the variety of criminal codes internationally. But a constant return to the general principle, do not kill, is an essential corollary of the right to life. The rights to *property* and *liberty* are separate and distinguishable from the right to life, but subordinate to it—for example, an agent who threatens us with some

---

[37] Albert Schweitzer, *The Teaching of Reverence for Life*, trans. Richard and Clara Winston (New York: Holt, Rinehart, and Winston, 1965), 26.

loss of freedom, or a loss of property which is not life-threatening, does not *ipso facto* forfeit his or her right to life.

Most people are not familiar with the term, "natural law." But it is probable that many, perhaps most, persons are implicitly aligned with one of the three types of natural law discussed in this chapter. Those with firm religious or theistic moorings may hold to natural law in the strict sense, motivated by the Gospels and the Ten Commandments, rather than any ethical theory. Others may go beyond the shifting trends of opinion polls to look seriously for a global perspective, basic moral values that we share with other generations and other cultures. Still others, without committing themselves to a "scientific" ethics, à la Bentham or Dewey, may consider the human and humane impulses, interactions and polarities that they experience, equally as authoritative and law-like as the scientific "laws" to which we are all subject.

8

Natural Law and
Contemporary Issues

*The belief that one has a determinate nature makes the injunction
to live in accordance with it imperative, at least if that nature can
be specified in some detail. The problem is thus not merely whether
one has a nature of this kind, but whether it can be known in
sufficient detail. The shortcoming of natural law theory is therefore
its typical failure to go beyond the insistence that human nature is
rational nature.*

— STEPHEN BUCKLE[1]

*If the trumpet give an uncertain sound, who shall prepare himself
for battle?*

— ST. PAUL, *First Corinthians* 14:8

One could argue that ethical theories come as an afterthought, generalizing extant thought patterns and practices. For example, utilitarian theory may simply be an attempt to spell out how most people who are considered ethical make their ethical decisions; Good Reasons theories similarly would describe the process that many people go through implicitly or explicitly in making moral judgments; and emotivism might be an attempt, after the fact, to distill the

---

[1] "Natural Law," in Peter Singer, ed., *A Companion to Ethics* (Cambridge: Blackwell, 1991).

essence of what goes on in ethical decision-making. One might also question whether anyone, except possibly an extremely cerebral philosopher, comes habitually to decisions on the basis of an ethical theory— for example, actually applying Kant's Categorical Imperative to decide whether one can borrow something without any intention of returning it, or actually applying natural-law theory to decide whether one has an obligation to support one's children. Possibly in most cases this sort of process goes on implicitly. But if an ethical theory is to be *normative*, in the strict sense, it should be available to supply directives at junctures where the more complex issues of right and wrong surface.

Natural law, according to some interpretations, should be indeterminate enough to cut a broad swath. For example, George Wright touts the indeterminacy of natural law as a virtue, and argues that extremely determinate natural law theories— "Gallup polls of moral facts"—are less plausible than theories that merely indicate a few general directive values, such as the natural law about respect for persons that led Oskar Schindler to disobey Nazi laws regarding the Jews.[2] And the attempts of Hobbes, Suarez, and others to give a more or less complete listing of natural-law applications paved the way for Bentham's observation about the arbitrariness of natural law. On the other hand, natural law should be determinate enough to give direction, even for contemporary problem-solving.

Most people now do not need natural law for instruction regarding clear-cut issues like genocide, slavery, or sexual molestation. But the fact that these issues are "clear-cut" seems to be a tribute to the fact that at a certain juncture in history, at least implicit natural-law considerations were influential in bringing about new moral insights and changing prevailing practices. In our own era, controversial moral problems exist, sometimes intermingled with issues peripheral to morality, which are susceptible of clarification by natural law. Examples of possible applications or implications of natural law regarding contemporary issues follow.

---

[2] R. George Wright, "Is Natural Law Theory of Any Use in Constitutional Interpretation?" *Law &: Southern California Interdisciplinary Law Journal* (1995), 463–487.

Abortion

Abortion is particularly difficult to address morally, since the moral issues are tightly intertwined with political, legal, and religious considerations. In a democratic political system, a substantial consensus on moral issues is a prerequisite in order to govern effectively; if, for example, the majority of citizens in the United States still favored slavery, an Emancipation Proclamation would be "whistling in the wind." In terms of legal structures, the enforceability of a law is of prime importance, as the United States discovered with Prohibition laws in the 1930s; and it goes without saying that without broad-based citizen support laws against abortion might require the massive intelligence network and the material and manpower resources of a police state in order to be enforced. Religious considerations are relevant also: one who believes that the human fetus or embryo has an immortal soul may be motivated to go beyond what seems to be permissible morally.

If we focus on the strictly ethical issues relevant to abortion, we notice first of all that a natural-law theory may lead to different conclusions than other ethical theories. A utilitarian approach, geared to maximizing happiness and minimizing pain for the greatest number of people, may countenance abortion in cases where favorable consequences can be predicted for the woman having the abortion, or the avoidance of painful consequences for the individual or society is predictable. A Kantian approach, requiring universalization of maxims and the avoidance of self-serving exceptions, would probably lead to the rejection of abortion; possibly most relevant would be Kant's "second formulation" of the Categorical Imperative: namely, that humanity in oneself or in any other person must always be treated as an end, never as a means to an end. A Humean approach, requiring the coordination of reason and emotions, would probably lead to variable conclusions, depending on the strength of sympathy or empathy for the unborn human, on the part of the person making the decision.

A natural-law approach, however, would emphasize sexual responsibility. This would lead immediately to conceptual and semantic hurdles. "Reproductive rights" now often connotes just the opposite of reproducing—the right to abort. "Sexual responsibility" has also taken on some specific meanings that are at variance with a natural-law definition. For many, the term, sexual responsibility, now connotes "safe sex"—the use of condoms—or combating overpopulation by the use of contraceptives or abortion. But the natural law of sexual responsibility emphasizes responsibility in the usual sense of the word—taking responsibility for one's choices, including the choice of sexual encounters.

But choice implies voluntariness. What about involuntary sexual intercourse? In cases of rape, the condition of sexual responsibility, as defined above, seems to fall by the wayside. A natural-law perspective on such cases would seem to differ from some other ethical approaches. Natural law can give no clear indication of duties in a situation where a woman has been forcibly impregnated. To be forced not only to bring the resultant pregnancy to term, let alone bring up the offspring of the rapist goes beyond the parameters of the natural, and even provides an illustrative *counterexample* of the confluence of the natural and the moral.

Cases of rape are best understood as paradigmatic conflicts between natural law and natural rights. As was mentioned above, the propagation of the species is a unique area where natural right and duty converge—humans have a duty to their own offspring, but also the right to give birth to their *own* offspring.[3] The natural right to propagate implies that a woman *chooses* to have intercourse that could result in her becoming pregnant. Any natural law governing reproduction would lose its force if it were not conjoined with the natural right of *voluntary* reproduction. A mother's natural reproductive right could take precedence over any *strict* duty to bear an embryo forcibly implanted. The type of duty that would be relevant to such cases is, to borrow Kantian terminology, supererogatory duty, or "laxer" duty. In other words, carrying a pregnancy from a forced sexual encounter to term would be commendable and admirable; but no strict obligation to do so is implied by the natural law, although other considerations, including religious motivations, such as the belief in fetal ensoulment, may very likely lead one to go beyond what is required.

Incestuous relationships usually involve rape, but are so universally considered unnatural as well as immoral and illegal, that it would be strange to speak of a "natural-law obligation" to carry incestuous pregnancies to full term. But here again, considerations of supererogatory duty or religious commitments may "trump" issues

---

[3] On natural and human rights, see pages 112ff above. On the convergence of rights and duties, see page 109.

of strict duty. It is intuitively clear that abortion on demand, as a means of contraception after normal and voluntary intercourse, is contrary to natural law; but in cases of abnormal or involuntary intercourse, natural law reaches the limits of intuitivity, and supplementary considerations may be called into play.

Natural-law theorists very often argue against all abortion from the principle enjoining respect for life.[4] But respect for life is a very broad value, applying conceivably to human and sub-human life, combatants and noncombatants, aggressors and non-aggressors, terminally ill patients and healthy persons, felons and law-abiding citizens. The application of this important and commendable value to specific situations in which abortion is contemplated is, again, not intuitive, but requires, as Suarez would put it, a process of "reflection." In cases such as ectopic gestation, in which the life of the mother or the fetus is threatened by the development of the fetus, the most relevant natural law could be the right to self-preservation rather than sexual responsibility. The deliberations here are more complex, since the degrees of a threat to life for both mother and fetus have to be weighed, and often are not easily predictable. In the event of a mortal threat to the mother, it would be consistent with the law of self-preservation for the mother to undergo procedures at an early stage that indirectly obviate the pregnancy, in order to preserve her life. If a mother chooses to risk her life to facilitate the possible survival of an infant, this choice would go beyond even the level of supererogatory duty to heroic virtue. But no strict duty to make such a choice (which might leave the infant without a mother to raise it) is clearly entailed by natural law.

A constitutional amendment recognizing the fetus as a legal person would make all abortion illegal, but entails problems of enforceability. A less comprehensive approach, not disdaining natural-law principles, might envision Congress making a law prohibiting abortion, but allowing exceptions only in cases of rape, incest, and threats to the life of the mother. Such a law would in effect supersede *Roe v. Wade*. The legal precedent for such constitutional supersession of the judiciary by the legislative power would be the 1862 congressional

---

[4] Cf. for instance the discussions of abortion by William May and Terry Hall, in David Forte, ed., *Natural Law and Contemporary Public Policy* (Washington, D.C.: Georgetown University Press, 1998): pp. 48, 147–48.

statute during the Lincoln administration simply ignoring the *Dred Scott* decision of the Supreme Court, which had declared slavery legal and Negroes non-citizens.

In vitro fertilization is connected with the issue of abortion, insofar as a couple will typically produce a large supply of frozen embryos as a prelude to implantation, with the hope of a successful pregnancy. But even after the successful pregnancy or pregnancies, the responsibility of deciding what to do with any remaining embryos lies with the couple. Adoption is hard to arrange and not usually a real option. To sanction the destruction of a human embryo even for research purposes differs procedurally from destruction of a fetus but conceptually only involves abortion at the earliest possible stage, like an abortifacient contraceptive.

Contraception

Contraception offers us still another example of an issue in which legal and religious aspects are intertwined with the moral aspects, and very difficult to separate. The religious barriers to contraception in the U.S. began to be removed in 1930 when the Anglican Lambeth Conference reversed the traditional Anglican position regarding the marital use of contraceptives; this was followed by the 1931 approval of the "careful and restrained" use of contraceptives by a committee of the Federal Council of Churches in March, 1931. The moral shock that these developments elicited in the public at that time was exemplified by official reactions from the Methodist, Presbyterian, Baptist, and Lutheran churches, as well as the Catholic Church—summed up in a March 22, 1931 editorial in the *Washington Post*:

> It is impossible to reconcile the doctrine of the divine institution of marriage with any modernistic plan for the mechanical regulation or suppression of human birth. The church must either reject the plain teachings of the Bible or reject schemes for the "scientific" production of human souls. Carried to its logical conclusion, the committee's report if carried into effect would sound the death-knell of marriage as a holy institution, by establishing degrading practices which would encourage indiscriminate immorality. The suggestion that the use of legalized contraceptives would be "careful and restrained" is preposterous.

The legal barriers to the sale of contraceptive devices in certain parts of the United States came down in the early 1960s with the Supreme Court's decision *Griswold v. Connecticut*. In the mid-1960s, Pope Paul VI's encyclical letter, *Humanae vitae*, proposed religious, as well as moral disincentives to the use of artificial birth-control methods—eliciting not only widespread controversy among moralists, but also a crisis with regard to ecclesiastical authority in moral matters. The Pope's moral arguments against contraception were based on a traditional Thomistic approach to natural law, and focused on the separation of sexuality from reproduction as a major infraction in the natural order. The "safe period" method, approved in the Encyclical, was at first pejoratively called "Vatican roulette" because of difficulties of determining ovulation with accuracy, but is no longer subject to such uncertainty for most couples with the use of proper methods. Current versions now approximate the less than 100-percent security of other methods of birth control. "Natural family planning" (NFP) methods, such as the Billings Ovulation Method, the Sympto-Thermal Method, and the Standard Days Methods, are considered morally acceptable, because they are naturally nonprocreative, but not antiprocreative. The *knowledge* of ovulation states in NFP (which is also important for infertile couples who want to have children) is not in the same category as a contraceptive block.

In many quarters now, contraception is no longer considered a moral issue, and even Catholic moralists are divided on the question. As mentioned above,[5] soon after the Pope's pronouncement, Grisez, Finnis, and other proponents of what is now known as the "new natural law theory" came to the Pope's defense, taking strong positions against the use of contraceptives even in marriage. Using hindsight, and focusing on the facts, we see that in the last few decades, with the rapid development of the contraceptive pill and other technical improvements, a *de facto* separation of sexuality from reproduction has indeed taken place in our culture. The inevitable corollary of this development has been the separation of sexuality from marriage as the main reproductive institution. "Recreational sex" in many forms is now widely considered to be "natural"—the major deterrent now being sexually transmitted disease, no longer social ostracism or the stigma of immorality.

---

[5] See above, pages xiv–xv, 104.

If sexual responsibility means accepting offspring, a major *dis*in-centive to such acceptance is the Malthusian theory of population, still held by some as scientific, in spite of the fact that its predictions, like the predictions of Marxism, have been completely falsified.[6] Neo-Malthusianism, along with kindred crusades against "overpopula-tion," has brought about a sea-change in the environment for sexual ethics.[7] According to the moral principles derived from the overpop-ulation perspective, humanity's new responsibility, *pace* the natural law and the divine law to "increase and multiply" from *Genesis,* is to *avoid* having children. This new "law" applies especially to poor peo-ple, and also makes it acceptable and even meritorious for rich as well as poor to engage in non-procreative sexual practices between "con-senting adults." But any sexual union in which reproductive possibil-ities are explicitly prevented would be a diremption of the natural order with regard to sexuality.

The natural-law approach emphasizes the objective connection between sexuality and reproduction, but intentions are also signifi-cant. Thus Finnis, with regard to the question of infertile couples, indicates that the important criterion is whether or not there is a "contralife" intention; someone intending to marry only an infertile spouse would be culpable.[8] But from a natural-law perspective, unin-tended infertility in such cases is morally unproblematic.

Homosexuality

Ethical questions about homosexuality have to be distinguished at the outset from aesthetic, legal, and political or administrative aspects. From a subjective vantage point, the aesthetic aspects are probably the most important. The reactions of many heterosexuals to sodomy as unaesthetic, disgusting, and ugly is difficult for individual heterosexuals to disengage from, whatever ethical judgments they may make about homosexuality; but attempts should be made to do this, in the interests of objectivity, just as a person finding someone

---

[6] See above, page 105.
[7] See above, *ibid.*
[8] See Ronald Garet, "Deposing Finnis," Law &: Southern California Interdisciplinary Law Journal 4:3 (Summer 1995).

physically unattractive should avoid extrapolating this feeling into a value judgment.

It is also important, prior to further discussion, to distinguish homosexuality from bisexuality. It is estimated that the majority of those who would classify themselves as homosexual are really bisexual, while only one to two percent of the population are "pure" homosexuals. When, for example, a man with several biological children discovers in his midforties that he is really "gay," the issue in such cases seems to be not homosexuality but bisexuality. The natural-law viewpoint with regard to these cases would emphasize not only possibly overriding obligations to one's children, but also the necessity for prioritizing one's heterosexual inclinations over whatever homosexual inclinations one has. At least the bisexual cannot claim a handicap or disadvantage in not being physically capable of normal sexual relationships.

It is not at present clear whether there are true biological homosexuals; an anomaly or exception to "normality" in the natural order could be considered a handicap, but is not "unnatural" in any moral sense. Studies of identical twins who have been raised separately, in which one twin is homosexual, have been inconclusive. And a Canadian study failed to replicate the "gay gene" discovery by Dr. Dean Hamer in 1993.[9] The American Psychiatric Association for many decades characterized homosexuality as a mental-health problem conditioned more by environmental factors (such as conflict with father figures) than by biological factors, but after intensive homosexual lobbying made a radical change of classification in 1973, to "normality," although section 302.9 of the APA diagnostic manual of mental disorders still allows for therapeutic assistance for "distressed" gays who are motivated to change their sexual orientation. (Dr. Robert Spitzer, who persuaded the American Psychiatric Association in 1973 to stop classifying homosexuality as a mental disorder, in recent years completed a five-year study of 200 homosexuals—143 males and 57 females—and concluded that homosexuals can change their sexual preference. He presented the results of his study on May 9th, 2001, at the annual meeting of the American Psychiatric Association.)

The "jury is still out" with regard to scientific proof of biological homosexuality. But studies of animals cast doubt on the possibility of such a state, if indeed humans have evolved from the primates. Cases

---

9 See Ingrid Wickelgren, "Discovery of 'Gay Gene' Questioned," *Science* 284:5414 (23rd April, 1999), 571.

of homosexual play and homosexual overtures are observed among animals prevented by circumstances from mating; but no evidence, with proper controls, is forthcoming of animals born without any instinct for heterosexual mating. But even if definitive proof of pure biological homosexuality among animals does finally emerge, this would have no necessary implications concerning what is natural or moral for humans, any more than recent evidence that higher primates do sometimes kill members of their own species.

Fears by heterosexuals concerning the possibility of pedophilia by teachers in schools and other institutions seem unwarranted, unless an individual homosexual is known to be a pederast, or unless evidence is forthcoming that homosexuals are significantly more likely than heterosexuals to become pedophiles. Fears of damaged morale or seduction in the military because of the induction of homosexuals may be legitimate, for the same reason that heterosexuals of both sexes sleeping and showering together in military units might be an impediment to discipline or morale. The same observation would be applicable to other cases where typically members of the same sex are living at close quarters—such as all-male seminaries or monasteries. In situations where adults are present at close quarters with children, the same standards should apply to homosexuals as to heterosexuals. If, for example, parents would not want heterosexual counselors of the opposite sex sleeping or showering at Boy Scout or Girl Scout camps with their children, it would be consistent and non-discriminatory to oppose homosexual counselors of the same sex as the children in similar situations.

Cohabitation

A natural-law approach to sex and marriage would be in some respects more liberal than contemporary mores, and in other respects more conservative. In contemporary culture, "living together" and contraception are typically interconnected; but fornication in which the intention would be to take responsibility for any resulting offspring would not be obviously contrary to natural law, as Grotius seemed to recognize.[10] And polygamous unions in which the care of progeny can be assured would also seem to be in conformity with natural law,

---

[10] See above, page 32. John Dedek, in his survey of forty-four theologians from 1152 to 1327, "Premarital Sex: The Theological Argument from Peter Lombard to

according to Grotius.[11] Aquinas argues that polyandry would not assure proper care of progeny, and thus is contrary to the natural law; but polygyny is not incompatible with the primary end of marriage, the care of children, although it tends to compromise the secondary end of marriage, the collaboration and harmony between the spouses.[12] Christianity traditionally "goes the extra mile," emphasizing monogamy, and Catholicism characterizes matrimony as the only sacrament administered not by a priest or other external minister, but by the marrying couples themselves. But it should be noted that in early Christianity bigamy seems to have been tolerated. For example, St. Paul in his epistle to Timothy admonishes Timothy[13] that bishops and deacons should be "husbands of one wife"—interpreted by some Scripture scholars as an admonition against widowers remarrying, but by other Scripture scholars as a special requirement of monogamy, not applicable to all classes of Christians; and Thomas Aquinas mentions that since bigamy is not prohibited by natural law, but only by positive laws, the Pope can dispense from the prohibition for ordained ministers, in certain cases.[14]

Strictly from a natural-law perspective, cohabitation, like polygamy, would not be prohibited, as long as there were no contra-life intention and as long as the union was intended to be permanent. In this case cohabitation would be tantamount to "common-law" marriage. But, as with polygamy, there are legal, political and economic drawbacks, as well as religious objections, to institutionalizing cohabitation—questions about uncertainty of offspring in non-exclusive sexual relationships, significant tendency of marriages after cohabitation to break up, relative impoverishment of single mothers after such breakups, disadvantages in education for children in such circumstances, and so on. Thus this issue may serve as a good example of the fact that it may be necessary for many reasons to go beyond what the natural law dictates.

Durand," *Theological Studies* 41:4 (December 1980), shows that, although there is consensus about the sinfulness of "simple fornication," there is considerable dispute as to whether it is relevant to natural law, to positive law, or to the laws of God revealed in the Scriptures.

[11] See above, page 35.

[12] *ST*, Supplement q.65, a.1.

[13] I *Timothy* (3:2, 12)

[14] *ST*, Supplement, q. 66, a.5c.

Assisted Suicide

The issue of physician-assisted suicide, hotly debated during the 1990s in Washington, Oregon, New York, and other states, led to a June 1997 decision by the Supreme Court that the ban of assisted suicide in states such as Washington and New York was constitutional, but that the state of Oregon was within its rights in permitting assisted suicide under tightly controlled conditions.[15] In other words, the issue has become a states-rights issue, largely dependent on the strength of opinions pro and con in the fifty states. Amid much legal discussion concerning the controversial right to privacy,[16] the Fourteenth Amendment, and liberty provisions of the Constitution, no final unambiguous legal decision applicable to the United States has been forthcoming; so that the issue has become a good example of permissible diversity within a democratic political system—decisions of state legislatures being influenced by lobbies and interest groups, and by public support or lack of such support. Questions about how seriously ill a patient must be to request euthanasia, and frequent questions about whether extreme depression should be a factor, whether the pain is manageable, whether relatives may be directly or indirectly influencing the patient to cease being a "burden," and so forth, make it difficult to formulate a clear-cut satisfactory legal decision on the matter.

If the moral aspects are disentangled, however, the issue is less ambiguous. Natural law promotes self-preservation and the worth of each individual to society. However, the duty to preserve oneself is not absolute. In a terminal disease with extreme pain, for example, the patient does not have to ask for or consent to extreme artificial meth-

---

[15] On Nov. 6, 2001, Attorney General John Ashcroft issued a directive indicating that assisted suicide was not a legitimate medical purpose, and that physicians intentionally prescribing drugs to kill a patient can face revocation of license to prescribe drugs. A court battle ensued and the issue may end up in the Supreme Court.

[16] "Controversial" because it seemed to be affirmed in the 1965 *Griswold v. Connecticut* decision, which overturned a Connecticut state law prohibiting use of contraceptives by married couples; but it has been challenged by the Supreme Court because of dubious constitutional grounds. In the successful reaffirmation of *Roe v. Wade* in the 1992 *Planned Parenthood of Southeastern Pennsylvania v. Casey*, the majority of justices based their decision on the Fourteenth Amendment rather than on the right of privacy.

ods for preserving life, and may refuse to eat or receive intravenous feeding. Physicians in such cases, where the will of the patient is clear, can withhold "disproportionate" artificial means, and even "pull the plug" where necessary, or use the pain medication which is necessary, even if it is so strong as to indirectly hasten the death of the patient. In cases of coma, the use of intravenous feeding, antibiotics, and other medications would not be in the category of extreme artificial measures, as long as there is hope for recovery. But *directly* killing a patient is not only complicity in the self-destructive act, but also a violation of the natural law against killing the innocent, not to mention inconsistent with the restriction about directly causing death in the Hippocratic Oath—now administered only intermittently to graduates of medical schools, and often taken with a "grain of salt" by the new physicians who do take it. Russell Hittinger[17] also makes the point that the transference of the right of using lethal force to the state, according to the social contract, would be abrogated with physician-assisted suicide, administered not by the state, but by private professional individuals without due-process, and would amount to a reversion from a state of political order to the state of nature.

Terrorism

It may seem strange and superfluous to include terrorism as a controversial moral issue to which natural-law theory might be applicable. Offhand, terrorism seems to fit into the same category as cannibalism, incest and infanticide—a category of behavior that is so obviously unnatural that no rational person would attempt to justify it or defend it. For if terrorism is defined as the indiscriminate killing of innocent, non-combatant men, women and children, for political or military purposes, 1) there is clearly no argument for self-defense that can be mustered by the terrorist; 2) if terrorism is extended to an entire nation or ethnic or religious group, the genocidal intent clearly is incompatible with any natural law of preserving the species; in addition, 3) suicide bombers go directly against the natural law of self-preservation; and, 4) perhaps most importantly, any kind of

---

[17] Russell Hittinger, *The First Grace* (Wilmington: ISI Books, 2003), Chapter 6.

terrorism is a manifestation of irrationality and misanthropy in the extreme.

But the mind of a terrorist proceeds along a very different path from all this. A terrorist act is construed by the terrorist as self-defense against a nation or group that has to be obliterated for one's own people to survive; even the children of the enemy are legitimate targets, since as they grow and propagate they will become an insuperable threat. For example, Palestinian terrorists considering themselves exiled from their homeland and subjugated to Israel, may consider it not irrational, but a rational long-range strategy, to kill Israeli women and children, as well as the citizens of any country essential to the support of Israel.

But unless would-be liberators are born without any ethical sensibility, we can presume that many of them will have qualms about indiscriminate murder, with or without self-destruction. And it is at this juncture that the *religious* factor becomes important. For even the most fundamental and natural ideas about wrongness can be overcome by the conviction of a divine command. Examples of this are readily available in the Hebrew Bible. The patriarch Abraham is willing to slay his son Isaac because of a divine command,[18] until receiving a last-minute reprieve through an angel; and Joshua and other Hebrew warriors are divinely commanded to slay men, women, children, and sometimes even the animals of their enemies.[19] In Islam, Imams who are considered successors of Mohammed are seen as imparting divine commands, sometimes offering interpretations of the *Koran* offering incentives for violent *jihad* or genocide campaigns. Christianity, with its "love your enemies" and "turn the other cheek" messages, does not easily give grounds for indiscriminate murder of enemies, but there are no limits to the power of individuals to distort the teachings even of a "religion of love."

The problem of such terrorists as suicide bombers is rooted in religion; and the solution to problems of this sort is to be found not in ethics but in religion. Only the authoritativeness of a divine mandate could override the instinctive humanity that we may presume is oper-

---

[18] *Genesis* 22. See my *Ethics in Context*, 122, for a discussion of this narrative.

[19] *Deuteronomy* 3:2, 7:2–5, 20:16; *Numbers* 2:34, 3:3; *Joshua* 6:21, 8:26–28, 11:20; see also I *Samuel* 15:3, 28:18; II *Samuel* 21. See my article, "Biblical Terrorism: With a Platonic Deconstruction," *Philosophy and Rhetoric* 32 (1999).

ative in the vast majority of persons. Abandonment of religious terrorism by a person of conscience may require abandonment of the religion supporting, or allegedly supporting, that terror.

Affirmative Action

Thomas Jefferson's affirmation in the Declaration of Independence that "all men are created equal" was presumably inspired by the natural-law theory of John Locke, which emphasized the natural and inalienable liberty of every human being. Obviously neither Locke nor Jefferson claimed, contrary to all appearances, an equality in physical or mental attributes for all human beings, but rather a more fundamental type of equality, leading members of a free society to avoid placing avoidable restrictions on the liberty of any individual. The fact that Jefferson himself did not implement this basic principle by freeing the slaves which he owned is an apparent inconsistency, still fraught with controversy, perhaps partially explainable by the difficulty faced by any individual in raising himself above the ingrained political, economic, and cultural institutions of his time. But natural law, whether the Lockean or other versions emphasizing the social nature of rational beings, would indicate that in a society where there are significant inequalities, steps should be taken to overcome such inequalities. "Equality of opportunity," frequently cited as an equalization stratagem, obviously must be interpreted according to the state and structure of society, but at a bare minimum would require not only mechanisms for legal redress of inequalities, but also economic incentives or disincentives in order to address economically-conditioned inequalities.

"Affirmative action" as a means of addressing inequalities of minorities and women in education, in the workplace, in promotions, in remuneration, living arrangements, etc., is characterized pejoratively by its opponents as social engineering, and by its proponents as the predictable response of a truly democratic society. But even proponents must agree that it is essentially a temporary response to the perceived inequalities, and that, if and when approximations to greater equality take place, it may be de-emphasized or discontinued. "Quotas" would be indicated only if there are extreme inequalities, along with resistance on the part of the perpetrators to any change in the *status quo*—especially in such areas as college admissions policies and long-standing preferential hiring practices of businesses and corporations. In the final analysis, natural law offers us some guidelines for minimizing harm in society, but no blueprint for constructing a utopia.

Stem-cell Research

Progress in stem-cell research has opened up a veritable Pandora's box of ethical problems. As more and more "lines" are developed, we are faced with literally hundreds of thousands of pluripotent stem cell lines, obtained from human embryos, aborted fetuses, and also by somatic cell nuclear transfer (SCNT). (SCNT has been carried out successfully in animals and in humans, presumably producing in effect the equivalent of a human embryo, which could develop into a blastocyst from which an inner cell mass could be extracted, if fetal development did not take place.) Scientists, ethicists, and political leaders may find themselves confronted with numerous stem-cell lines obtained by questionable methods, and be told, "we've got to use them while they're viable and available."

In recent experiments with animals, stem cells have been obtained from unfertilized eggs (oocytes) through chemically-induced parthenogenesis. If a similar procedure could be used to derive stem cells from humans, contra-life objections to their use for clinical procedures would not be avoided, since such cells could be in effect imperfect human beings, for whom science has not yet found procedures for development beyond the blastocyst stage.

No moral issue would seem to exist if stem cells were obtained from umbilical cords, miscarriages, or adults. Specialized (not pluripotent, but multipotent) stem cells, for blood and neural tissue, for cardiac tissue (which might be useful for heart disease), or pancreatic tissue (with possible use for insulin production in diabetes) have been found in adults, and adult stem cells have been used to treat Parkinson's disease and leukemia; many other potential therapeutic uses exist. With extraction and use of these multipotent cells, there is less danger of immune responses causing tissue rejection or tumors, when adult multipotent stem cells are obtained from the person being treated.

But, even if stem cells for all types of specialized uses could be found in adults, the production from embryos is preferred by many practitioners because it offers less complex access to pluripotent cells, which might be redirected to all types of specialized functions, possibly offering the most accessible cures for Parkinson's disease, Alzheimer's disease, spinal cord injury, burns, and other conditions. The problem of possible tissue rejection from transplanted cell lines obtained from embryos has not yet been solved, but scientists are optimistic about overcoming this hurdle. Scientists are also optimistic about the possibility of modifying the pluripotent cells into multipotent cells for special functions. Thus the main arguments favoring embryonic stem cell production are utilitarian: the lines are easier to obtain and culture for various uses, and no long waiting would be necessary when stem cells are needed for implantation in acute situations.

The political issues should be distinguished from the moral issues with regard to stem-cell research. Political decisions in a democracy, where wide consensus is necessary, can permit practices which many deem immoral—such as prostitution or abortion—especially where prohibitions would be unenforceable. *De facto* embryos were destroyed (for example in experiments by Dr. James Thompson), and some aborted fetuses were used to produce stem cells (for instance in Dr. Gearhart's experiments). The decision by the Bush administration to allow research on stem-cell lines already obtained by destruction of embryos was a compromise influenced in large part by political considerations, since contrary public opinion would have made an absolute prohibition difficult. In March, 2002, the National Institutes of Health determined that federally financed researchers could indeed study new stem cell lines — and even derive them from embryos—in their university laboratories, provided that they do not commingle their federal and private money.

The connection of stem cell research with *in vitro* fertilization and abortion is of course objectionable from the viewpoint of natural law. The recourse to *in vitro* fertilization or aborted embryos to obtain the cell lines puts the practice in the category of "ends justifying the means." It should be noted that sixteen countries—including Germany, Austria, France, Switzerland, Norway, Ireland, Brazil, Peru and Poland—have prohibited the creation of embryos specifically for the purpose of stem cell research. In European Union deliberations in December, 2003, Germany, Austria and Italy vetoed a proposal to use EU funds for embryonic stem cell research.

"Political Correctness"

In contemporary usage, "political correctness" (PC) is an umbrella term, applied pejoratively to concerted attempts by individuals or groups to impose a specific way of acting or thinking on others. The culprits exerting such pressure on others are typically categorized as political liberals, or liberally oriented universities, or liberal institutions or think-tanks; but one can envision conservative forms also— for example the pressure on Republicans by fellow Republicans to be against "big government" or for tax cuts or against restrictions on business or investors. The claim is that PC goes beyond any of the multifarious forms of social pressure we are all familiar with—boys being pressured not to do anything girlish, teenagers to be "cool," adults to "keep up with the Joneses," and the like. PC is relevant to natural-law considerations only when it impinges on moral issues— not, for example, when it has to do with cultural objectives such as using "inclusive language," or redefining gender roles in career expectations, or promoting diversity, or bilingual education. But natural-law implications clearly turn up when a "litmus test" about holding certain moral positions is applied. Thus one who is against abortion or artificial contraception or homosexual practices could not, under the current rubric of PC, be considered a liberal, even if he or she is a staunch supporter of other liberal causes—equal opportunity, affirmative action, abolishing death penalty, prohibiting child labor, universal health insurance, separating church and state, freeing political prisoners, teaching of evolution, and so forth. The discriminatory results may take the form of not being hired on certain campuses, not being invited for speaking engagements or panel discussions, not being appointed to certain political offices or administrative positions, and so forth. The main symptom of PC in the moral sense is a complete unwillingness to investigate or even listen to arguments contrary to the chosen position. If the basic inclination of a rational being is to know the truth, even about moral matters, and if this implies an obligation to pursue the truth (as has been argued in this book), to redirect or stifle this natural inclination is contrary to natural law. This can become the democratic version of the "brainwashing" connected with totalitarian regimes, which have been able to use more overt, systematic and forcible methods for enforcing moral consensus.

Final Observation

The ethical theory we align ourselves with, implicitly or explicitly, is more important than the car we drive, the tools and methods we use, the multifarious rules we follow. A major danger is metaethical eclecticism—following whatever ethical principles give us the best advantage or serve our interests. Thus, as with changing fashions, one might use utilitarian deliberations when the issue is affirmative action or euthanasia, but deliberate in deontological fashion when the issue is abortion or cohabitation. As we have seen from the preceding examples, natural-law thinking will tend to conclusions that may diverge from the conclusions indicated by other ethical theories. In any case, one should not adopt a theory because it leads to preferred conclusions, but choose a theory because it offers a cogent, credible and consistent approach to moral thinking and moral problem-solving. Natural-law theorists, as we have seen, have become highly diversified. Some argue that natural-law theory must be grounded in an intellectually acceptable concept of nature, and bolstered by the presupposition of a Divinity sanctioning moral laws and rights; others eschew "metaphysical" presuppositions, but still look upon the "laws of human nature," especially the law of acting according to reason, as equal in importance and authoritativeness to the laws of physics or chemistry; others capitalize on global consensus concerning universal rights, and the duties corresponding to these rights. If we look for some "common denominator" amid these differences, what suggests itself is a desire to avoid relativism and to point out a certain bedrock of objective moral values capable of giving direction when questions such as those listed above occur. It is interesting that the present differences among natural lawyers are not primarily about the positions they hold on such issues, but about what is meant by natural law. The object of this book has been to clarify the tradition, to help unravel the current diversity of interpretations, and to show where they lead.

Bibliography

Aquinas, Thomas. *Commentary on Aristotle's Nicomachean Ethics*. Trans. C.I. Litzinger. Chicago: Regnery, 1964.

———. *Summa Theologica*. Three volumes, literally translated by Fathers of the English Dominican Province. New York: Benziger Brothers, 1947.

———. *In decem libros Ethicorum Aristotelis ad Nicomachum expositio* Thomae Aquinatis. Cura et studio Raymundi M.Spiazzi. Taurini: Marietti, 1949.

Aristotle. *Nicomachean Ethics*. Trans. W.D. Ross. In Richard McKeon, ed., *The Basic Works of Aristotle* (New York: Random House, 1941).

———. *Rhetorica*. Trans. W. Rhys Roberts. In Richard McKeon, ed., *The Basic Works of Aristotle* (New York: Random House, 1941).

———. *Politics*. Trans. Benjamin Jowett. In Richard McKeon, ed., *The Basic Works of Aristotle* (New York: Random House, 1941).

———. *De Anima*. Trans. J.A. Smith. In Richard McKeon, ed., *The Basic Works of Aristotle* (New York: Random House, 1941).

Arnhart, Larry. *Darwinian Natural Right: The Biological Ethics of Human Nature*. New York: State University of New York Press, 1998.

Aurelius, Marcus. *The Meditations of Marcus Aurelius Antonius*. Trans. George Long. Mount Vernon: Peter Pauper Press, 195?.

Bailey, Ronald. The Law of Increasing Returns. *The National Interest* 59 (Spring 2000), 113–121.

Barrow, John, and Frank Tipler. *The Anthropic Cosmological Principle*. New York: Oxford University Press, 1988.

Bauer, Peter, *Development Frontier: Essays in Applied Economics*. Cambridge, Massachusetts: Harvard University Press, 1991.

Baumrin, Bernard. Is There a Naturalistic Fallacy? *American Philosophical Quarterly* 5 (April 1968), 79–89.

Bentham, Jeremy. *An Introduction to the Principles of Morals and Legislation*, ed. J.H. Burns, and H.L.A. Hart. New York: Methuen, 1982

Biggar, Nigel, and Rufus Black, eds. *The Revival of Natural Law: Philosophical, Theological, and Ethical Responses to the Finnis-Grisez School.* Aldershot: Ashgate, 2000.

Black, Max. *The Is-Ought Question.* Ed. W.D. Hudson. Macmillan: London, 1969.

Bourke, Vernon. Is Thomas Aquinas a Natural Law Ethicist? *The Monist* 58 (1974), 52–66.

———. Finnis's *Natural Law and Natural Rights. American Journal of Jurisprudence* 26 (1981), 243–47.

Brown, Donald. *Human Universals.* Philadelphia: Temple University Press, 1991.

Brown, Raymond, et al. *The New Jerome Biblical Commentary.* Englewood Cliffs: Prentice Hall, 1990.

Burnet, John. *Early Greek Philosophy.* Cleveland: World Publishing Company, 1963.

Cicero, Marcus Tullius. *On the Republic.* Trans. Charles Duke Yonge. London: H.G. Bohn, 1853.

———. *On the Laws.* Trans. Charles Duke Yonge. London: H.G. Bohn, 1853.

———. *De Officiis.* Trans. Thomas Kockman. Irvine: World Library, 1991–1994.

Clark, Colin. *Population Growth: The Advantages.* Santa Ana: Sassone, 1972.

Covell, Charles. *The Defence of Natural Law.* New York: St. Martin's Press, 1992.

Copleston, Frederick. *History of Philosophy. Volume 5: Hobbes to Hume.* Westminster, Md: Newman Press, 1959.

Crowe, Michael. *The Changing Profile of the Natural Law.* The Hague: Nijhoff, 1977.

Cumberland, Richard. *Treatise of the Laws of Nature.* Trans. John Maxwell. Reprint of the 1727 edition. New York: Garland, 1978.

Cunningham, Stanley. Albertus Magnus on Natural Law. *Journal of the History of Ideas* 28 (October–December 1967), 479–502.

Curran, C., and R.A. McCormick, S.J., eds. *Readings in Moral Theology, no. 7.* New York: Paulist Press, 1991.

Dedek, John. Premarital Sex: The Theological Argument from Peter Lombard to Durand. *Theological Studies* 41:4 (1980).

Devine, Philip. *Natural Law Ethics.* Westport: Greenwood Press, 2000.

Dodd, Julian, and Suzanne Stern-Gillet. The Is-Ought Gap, the Fact-Value Distinction, and the Naturalistic Fallacy. *Dialogue* 34 (1995), 727–745.

Dworkin, Ronald. Morality and Law: Observations Prompted by Professor Fuller's Novel Claim. *University of Pennsylvania Law Review*, Vol. 113 (1965), 668–690.

Eberstadt, Nick. Population and Economic Growth. *Wilson Quarterly* 10:5 (Winter 1986).

Einar, Kenneth. Functionalism and Legal Theory: the Hart-Fuller Debate Revisited. *De philosophia* 14 (1998).

Epictetus. *The Golden Sayings of Epictetus.* Trans. Hastings Crossley. In Vol II of the Harvard Classics. New York: Collier, 1909.

Evans, Illtud, O.P. *Light on the Natural Law.* Baltimore: Helicon, 1965.

Ferris, Timothy. *The Whole Shebang.* New York: Simon and Schuster, 1997.

Finnis, John. *Natural Law and Natural Rights.* Oxford: Clarendon, 1980.

———. Natural Law and Unnatural Acts. *Heythrop Journal* 11 (1970), 365–387.

Forte, David F. *Natural Law and Contemporary Public Policy.* Washington, D.C.: Georgetown University Press, 1998.

Foster, John. *The Immaterial Self: A Defence of the Caresian Dualist Conception of the Mind.* London: Routledge, 1991.

Freud, Sigmund. *A General Introduction to Psychoanalysis.* Trans. Joan Rivière. Garden City: Garden City Publishers, 1943.

Fuller, Lon. *The Morality of Law.* New Haven: Yale University Press,1969.

Herdt, Jennifer. Free Choice, Self-Referential Arguments, and the New Natural Law. *American Catholic Philosophical Quarterly* 72 (1998), 581–600.

Garet, Ronald. Deposing Finnis. *Law &: Southern California Interdisciplinary Law Journal* 4 (Summer 1995), 605–652.

George, Robert. *In Defense of Natural Law.* New York: Clarendon, 1999.

Grisez, Germain. *The Way of the Lord Jesus.* Chicago: Franciscan Herald Press, 1983.

———. The First Principle of Practical Reason: A Commentary on the *Summa theologiae* I–II, qu. 94 art 2. *Natural Law Forum* 10 (1965), 168–196.

Grotius, Hugo. *De Jure Belli ac Pacis Libri Tres.* Trans. Francis Kelsey. New York: Oceana, 1964.

Guillermo of Auxerre. *Summa Aurea in quattuor libros sententiarum.* Unveraenderter Nachdruck. Frankfurt am Main: Minerva, 1964.

Hart, H.L.A. *The Concept of Law.* Oxford: Clarendon, 1961.

———. Philosophy of Law and Jurisprudence in Britain (1945–1952). *American Journal of Comparative Law* 2 (1953), 355–364.

———. Positivism and the Separation of Law and Morals. *Harvard Law Review* 71 (1957), 593–629.

Hegel, G.W.F. *Selections from Hegel's* Phenomenology of Spirit*: Bilingual Edition with Commentary.* Translated and Annotated by H.P. Kainz. University Park: Pennsylvania State University Press, 1994.

———. *The Philosophy of Right.* Trans. T.M. Knox. New York: Oxford University Press, 1967.

Henry, Carl. Natural Law and a Nihilistic Culture. *First Things* 49 (January 1995), 55–60.

Herdt, Jennifer. Free Choice, Self-Referential Arguments, and the New Natural Law. *American Catholic Philosophical Quarterly* 72 (August 98), 581–600.

Hittinger, Russell. *A Critique of the New Natural Law Theory.* Notre Dame: University of Notre Dame Press, 1987.

———. *The First Grace: Rediscovering the Natural Law in a Post-Christian World.* Wilmington: ISI Books, 2003.

Hirzel, Rudoph. *Agraphos Nomos.* New York: Arno, 1979.

Hobbes, Thomas. *De Cive.* Trans. Thomas Hobbes. Ed. Bernard Gert. Indianapolis: Hackett, 1991.

Hood, Francis. *The Divine Politics of Thomas Hobbes: An Interpretation of Leviathan.* Oxford: Clarendon, 1964.

Hume, David. *An Enquiry Concerning the Principles of Morals.* Indianapolis: Library of Liberal Arts, 1957.

———. *A Treatise of Human Nature.* Oxford: Oxford University Press, 2000.

Iamblichus. *Life of Pythagoras.* Trans. Thomas Taylor. London: John M. Watkins, 1965.

Kainz, Howard. *Ethics in Context: Towards the Definition and Differentiation of the Morally Good.* London: Macmillan/Washington, DC: Georgetown University Press, 1987.

———. Biblical Terrorism: With a Platonic Deconstruction. *Philosophy and Rhetoric* 32 (1999).

Kant, Immanuel. *Fundamental Principles of a Metaphysic of Morals.* Trans. Thomas Abbott. Indianapolis: Library of Liberal Arts, 1949.

———. *Introduction to a Metaphysic of Morals.* Trans. W. Hastie. New York: World Library, 1991.

Kerruish, Valerie. Philosophical Retreat: A Criticism of John Finnis's Theory of Natural Law. *University of Western Australia Law Review* 15 (1983), 224–244.

Kierkegaard, Søren. *Either/Or.* Trans. Walter Lowrie. New York: Anchor, 1959.

Kirk, G.S., and J.E. Raven, eds. *The Presocratic Philosophers.* Cambridge: Cambridge University Press, 1957.

Laymon, Charles, ed. *The Interpreter's One-Volume Commentary on the Bible.* Nashville: Abingdon, 1971.

Lisska, Anthony. *Aquinas's Theory of Natural Law.* Oxford: Clarendon, 1996.

Locke, John. *An Essay Concerning Human Understanding.* Oxford: Clarendon, 1979.

MacIntyre, Alasdair. Hume on 'Is' and 'Ought'. In W.D. Hudson, ed., *The Is-Ought Question* (London: Macmillan, 1969).

Maritain, Jacques. *Man and the State.* Chicago: University of Chicago Press, 1951.

Martinich, Aloysius. *The Two Gods of Leviathan: Thomas Hobbes on Religion and Politics.* New York: Cambridge University Press, 1992.

McDermott, John M., S.J. Love and the Natural Law. *Vera Lex* 9 (1989), 11–12.

McInerny, Ralph. *Aquinas on Human Action: A Theory of Practice.* Washington, D.C.: Catholic University of America Press, 1992.

———. *Ethica Thomistica: The Moral Philosophy of Thomas Aquinas.* Washington, D.C.: Catholic University of America Press, 1982.

McLean, Edward, ed. *Common Truths: New Perspectives on Natural Law.* Wilmington: ISI Books, 2000.

Miller, Fred, Jr. *Nature, Justice, and Rights in Aristotle's* Politics. Oxford: Clarendon, 1995.

Montesquieu, Charles. *The Spirit of the Laws.* Trans. Thomas Nugent. London: Bell, 1878.

Newton, Isaac. *Mathematical Principles of Natural Philosophy.* Chicago: Encyclopaedia Brittanica,1952.

Peters, F.E. *Greek Philosoophical Terms: A Historical Lexicon.* New York: New York University Press, 1967.

Plato. *The Dialogues of Plato.* Trans. B. Jowett. New York: Random House, 1937.

Pope Paul VI. *On the Regulation of Birth.* Washington, D.C.: United States Catholic Conference, 1968.

Porter, Jean. *Natural and Divine Law: Reclaiming the Tradition for Christian Ethics.* Grand Rapids: Eerdmans, 1999.

Pufendorf, Samuel. *On the Duty of Man and Citizen, according to Natural Law.* New York: Cambridge University Press, 1991.

Raphael, D. Daiches. *The Moral Sense.* London: Oxford University Press, 1947.

Rommen, Heinrich. *The Natural Law: A Study in Legal and Social History and Philosophy.* Trans. Thomas R. Hanley. St. Louis: Herder, 1947.

Scavone, Robert. Natural Law, Obligation, and the Common Good: What Finnis Can't Tell Us. *University of Toronto Faculty of Law Review* 43 (1985), 90–115.

Schockenhoff, Eberhard. *Natural Law and Human Dignity: Universal Ethics in an Historical World.* Washington, D.C.: Catholic University of America Press, 2003.

Schweitzer, Albert. *The Teaching of Reverence for Life.* Trans. Richard and Clara Winston. New York: Holt, Rinehart, and Winston, 1965.

Shaver, Robert. *Hobbes.* Aldershot: Ashgate, 1999.

Sheldrake, Rupert. *The Rebirth of Nature.* Rochester, Vt: Inner Traditions International, 1994.

Shermer, Michael. *In Darwin's Shadow: The Life and Science of Alfred Russel Wallace.* Oxford: Oxford University Press, 2002.

Sidgwick, Henry. *The Methods of Ethics.* London: Macmillan, 1963.

Simon, Julian. *Hoodwinking the Nation.* New Brunswick: Transaction, 1999.

Smith, Bruce, et al. *Technology, R&D, and the Economy.* Washington, D.C.: Brookings Institution, 1996.

Stewart, M.A., and John P. Wright, eds. *Hume and Hume's Connexions.* University Park: Pennsylvania State University Press, 1994.

Suarez, Francisco. *A Treatise on Laws and God the Lawgiver.* In James Brown Scott, ed., *Selections From Three Works by Francisco Suarez,* Vol. II (Oxford: Clarendon, 1944).

Taylor, A.E. The Ethical Doctrine of Hobbes. *Philosophy* 13 (1938).

Trewavas, Anthony. Malthus Foiled Again and Again. *Nature* 418 (2002).

Uniacke, Suzanne. Self Defense and the Natural Law. *American Journal of Jurisprudence* 36 (1991), 73–101.

Van den Haag, Ernest. Not Above the Law. *National Review* 43 (October 7th, 1991), 35–36.

Veatch, Henry B. Finnis's *Natural Law and Natural Rights. American Journal of Jurisprudence* 26 (1981), 247–259.

———. *Swimming Against the Current in Contemporary Philosophy.* Washington, D.C.: Catholic University of America Press, 1990.

Vitoria, Francisco. *De Indis et De iure belli: Relectiones.* Edited by Ernest Nys. New York: Oceana, 1964.

Wagner, Theresa, ed. *Back to the Drawing Board: The Future of the Pro-Life Movement.* South Bend: St. Augustine's Press, 2003.

Warrender, Howard. *The Political Philosophy of Hobbes: His Theory of Obligation.* Oxford: Clarendon, 1957.

Westerman, Pauline. *The Disintegration of Natural Law Theory: Aquinas to Finnis.* Leiden: Brill, 1998.

Wheelwright, Philip. *The Presocratics.* New York: Odyssey Press, 1966.

Wilson, James Q. *The Moral Sense.* New York: Free Press, 1993.

Wolf, Erik. *Das Problem der Naturrechtslehre: Versuch einer Orientierung.* Karlsruhe: Müller, 1955.

Wolfe, Chistopher. Judicial Review. In David Forte, ed., *Natural Law and Contemporary Public Policy* (Washington, D.C.: Georgetown University Press, 1998).

Wright, R. George. Is Natural Law Theory of Any Use in Constitutional Interpretation? *Law &: Southern California Interdisciplinary Law Journal* 4 (Summer 1995), 463–487.

Index

dovetails is-ought, 109–10
imbedding, 100
FBI, 84
Fichte, 76
Finnis, John, xiv, xiv (note), 46ff, 46,
    62n2, 65n, 73, 108
  and metaphysics, 49, 88
  basic values, 47ff, 81, 86
  criticisms of, 50–54
  new natural law theory, 46ff, 69,
    121
  on homosexuality and
    contraception, 104
  basic values, 47
First Corinthians, 115
First Samuel, 128n
First Timothy, 125, 125n
Food supplies, 105
Fornication, 124–25
Ford, John, S.J., xv (note)
Forte, David F., xii (note), 119
Foster, John, 66
Frankfurter, Justice Felix, 44
Freedom, self-determination, 108–9
Freud, Sigmund, 61, 61n
Friendship as basic value, 47
Fuller, Lon, xiii–xiv, xiv (note), 45,
    45n
Funding money, federal and private,
    stem cell research, 131

Gaia hypothesis, 58
Gaius, 15, 16
Galileo, 64, 100
Garet, Ronald, 122n
Gearhart, John D., Dr., Stem Cell
    Research Foundation, 131
Genesis, 128n
Genocide campaigns, 128
George, Robert, xv, xv (note)
Germany, stem cell research, 131
God as lawgiver, 39
Golden mean, 57, 108
Golden Rule, 16, 27, 110, 111
Gratian, 16
Gravity, 101

Greek literature and natural law, 1
Grisez, Germain, xiv, xv (note), 46,
    49, 50, 52, 53, 69, 121
Griswold vs Connecticut, 121, 126n
Grotius, Hugo, 31–34, 37n
  empirical natural law, 97–99
  fornication, 124
  natural-law connection with God,
    53, 88
  sanctions for natural law, 64, 83
  slavery, 89, 91
Guillermo of Auxerre, 22n
Guth, Alan, 101

Hall, Terry, 119
Happiness
  as good, Aristotle, 79
  fact-value and is-ought, 77
  in Aristotle, 56
Hart, H.L.A., xiv (note), 43, 43n, 45,
    45n, 46, 103
  immoral laws, xiii–xiv
Harvard Law Review, xiii
Heart disease, 130
Hebrew Bible, 94, 96, 103, 128
Hegel, G.W.F.
  criticism of Kantian morality,
    74–76, 82
  on the dialectic of rights and
    duties, 112
Henderson, Lawrence, 79–80
Henry, Carl, 89–90, 90n
  slavery, 89–90
Hentoff, Nat, 88, 88n
Heraclitus, 1
Herdt, Jennifer, 52, 52n
Hippias, 2–3
Hippocratic Oath, 127
Hirzel, Rudolf, 3n
Hittinger, Russell, xv, xv (note), 45,
    127, 127n
Hobbes, Thomas, 19, 34–36, 88,
    116
  ethical egoism, 37n
  laws of nature, 34–36, 64–65
  "state of nature" theory, 34, 103